CRICKET KATHAS

Fascinating stories from the cricket world.

MAHESH KUTTY

ISBN 979-8-88805-494-9

Contents

PREFACE

In our country, cricketers are revered as demigods, and the game is more of a religion than a sport. Needless to say, fans are yearning for anecdotes about cricketers both on and off the field. 'Cricket Kathas' is the ideal book for cricket enthusiasts. There are intriguing tales about several champion cricketers who inspired many of us to enjoy the game. The stories do not just feature Indian players, but also those from Australia, Pakistan, England, Sri Lanka, the West Indies and New Zealand.

Don Bradman is widely regarded as the greatest batsman in history, but only a few people are aware that he was also an exceptional billiards player. In fact, he vanquished World Champion Walter Lindrum without even giving him a chance.

Most of us who grew up watching cricket in the 1970s and 1980s wondered if Vivian Richards would have been successful against his own fast bowlers. Richards and Marshall once fought hard in a county match that will go down in history as one of the most epic battles in county cricket.

Nobody can dispute Sachin Tendulkar's brilliance, but how many of his ardent fans are aware that he once batted in the nets with his eyes closed?

These and other incredible stories are collected in 'Cricket Kathas.'

Acknowledgements

This book is dedicated to all cricket enthusiasts around the world.

The journey of writing this book began on January 1, 2022. It was a fantastic experience that broadened my understanding of our beautiful game. I have to admit that it would not have been possible without the help of family and friends.

My brother Manoj would call me every alternate day from the USA to check on my progress, and my father, a passionate cricket fan, would ask me for a story every time I went to see him. It just motivated me to complete the book.

My sincere thanks to Vishnu Govind, my partner in crime at KricketWicket, who served as an excellent sounding board for picking the stories. Thanks also to the Cherry & Timber Talk team – Devendra, Nishad, Venu and Yogi for enriching my cricket knowledge with in-depth cricket discussions.

Lastly, I would like to express my gratitude to Gangadharan Menon for carefully reading the book.

CHAPTER 1

THE DON OF CRICKET

One name that is taken with respect across the cricket world is Don Bradman. Having amassed 6996 runs in just 52 Test matches with an average of 99.94, Bradman's statistics is outrageously brilliant. He played most of his cricket against England and scored loads of runs against them. He played 5 Test matches each against West Indies, South Africa and India.

England were so petrified of Bradman that they devised the Bodyline attack – a strategy that was against the spirit of the game. No doubt, England enjoyed success as Bradman scored just one century in the Series with an average of 56.57. But otherwise Bradman did not have a lean patch during his entire career between 1930 and 1948.

Bradman made his debut in the first Test match of the 1928 Series against England at Brisbane. Unfortunately he did not have a memorable Test match as he managed to score only 18 and 1. Australia lost the match by 675 runs and Bradman was dropped for the second Test match at Sydney. In that match, Bradman was fielding as a substitute. Bradman was an extremely good fielder but sadly his fielding skills are never discussed, as all the attention is taken away by his batting. On one occasion he fielded the ball and threw it. The ball missed England opener Herbert Sutcliffe by a whisker and landed in the wicketkeeper's gloves. At the end of the over Sutcliffe asked Bradman "Hey young man, were you trying to hit me?" Bradman shot back a cryptic reply "When I try, I don't miss." For someone playing in his debut Series, this response indicates Bradman's supreme confidence and self belief.

Bradman had a unique way of honing his batting skill. He would practice for hours by hitting a golf ball against the wall with a stump. This he believed helped his hand-eye coordination and when he played with the cricket bat, the ball hit the sweet spot of the bat more often than not. He scored runs at a rapid pace; in fact he is the only batsman in the history of the game to have scored 300 runs in a day. Bradman believed that it was imperative to score runs quickly as it would give the bowlers enough time to bowl out the opposition twice. Though he was an aggressive batsman, he took minimum risk. Once Harold Larwood, Bradman's adversary in the Bodyline Series was asked to compare Bradman and the destructive Vivian Richards who was at the peak of his career. Larwood replied that Richards gave many chances for the opposition to get him out but Bradman would not give a single chance. And that made Bradman an exceptional batsman.

While Bradman was a genius with the bat, his skill on the billiards table was there for everyone to see. In 1934, Australia's billiards champion Walter Lindrum and Don Bradman decided to play a game. Lindrum beat him comprehensively. In fact it was a defeat where Lindrum cleaned up the table without giving Bradman a single shot. The defeat hurt Bradman and he decided to sharpen his game. So he practised and practised till he was ready to challenge Lindrum. When the two met for the return match, Bradman told Lindrum that it was only fair that he starts the game. Not aware of the improved skill of Bradman, Lindrum readily agreed. To his utter disbelief Bradman sank in every ball and reached 147 without allowing Lindrum to pick up the cue stick. The greatness of Bradman was that he relentlessly pursued his goals and achieved them.

On the eve of the 4th Test match at Leeds in the 1934 Series, Don Bradman and the famous English writer Sir Neville Cardus were having dinner. During the dinner, Bradman told Cardus that they should wind up early since he wanted to rest well and score big in the Test match the following day. To this, Cardus reminded Bradman that he had scored 334 in his earlier tour at Leeds so he would not be able to score heavily this time around. Bradman in a quizzical tone gently enquired why he would not score big. Cardus replied that the law of averages would deny him a big score. Bradman promptly replied in a confident tone that he did not believe in the law of averages. And he was dead right! He scored a masterful 304.

After a hard day on the field, some players loved to have a drink, some would party but Bradman would play Chopin for hours. He loved his music and preferred it over billiards and golf. Though he was a teetotaller during his playing days, he enjoyed whisky and wine after he turned 40; but like everything else he enjoyed it well.

Bradman's health reasons almost denied him from going to England for his last Series. Despite being 39 and not in the pink of health he travelled to England because the English spectators adored him and he loved them.

He scored an unbeaten 173 at Leeds in the second innings of the penultimate Test. He may well have scored four more runs but his partner Neil Harvey got a ball on his pads and he clipped it to the boundary. Had Bradman scored four more runs at Leeds, he would have finished his career at an astonishing average of 100 even with a duck at the Oval. Nobody knew about it!

England were bowled out for 52 runs on the first day of the last Test at the Oval. Australia reached 117 before Barnes was out. In walked Bradman with about 40 minutes of play left for the day. A packed stadium greeted the genius. The English players saluted his arrival at the crease by taking off their caps and giving him the customary 3 cheers. While there are reports that Bradman's eyes were moist, Bradman denies it. He says that the reception stirred his emotions and made him anxious. He so dearly wanted to do well but sadly got out for zero.

Eric Hollies, the leg spin googly bowler played against Bradman in the county match leading up to the final Test match. He felt that Bradman was not picking his googly in the first innings so he decided not to bowl a single googly in the second innings so that he could surprise Bradman just in case he was picked for the Oval Test match. He mentioned to his Warwickshire teammate that if he plays at the Oval, the second ball he bowls to Bradman would be a googly.

Bradman played the first ball defensively but says that he wasn't sure that he had really seen it. The last ball of

Bradman's illustrious career ended with the googly. Bradman lunged forward but the ball took the inside edge of the bat and hit the stumps. The genius was out for zero. Pin drop silence engulfed the Oval cricket ground. And then as he got closer to the pavilion, the spectators realised that he would never bat again in international cricket. The applause was deafening as Bradman slowly made his way back to the dressing room.

Watching the incredible farewell Bradman was getting, Eric Hollies told his teammates that he'd just bowled the best ball of his life but the applause was for Bradman. However Eric Hollies has a stand named after him at Edgbaston.

During India's tour to Australia in 1998, Sachin Tendulkar and Shane Warne were invited by Don Bradman on his 90th birthday on August 27th. Both Tendulkar and Warne were confident players and had dazzled the world with their skills but they were nervous of their meeting with the greatest batsman of all time. Tendulkar told Warne to start the conversation and then he would follow up. As they got a little comfortable, Tendulkar asked Bradman how much would he average if he was playing today? Bradman thought for about 10 seconds and replied "Maybe about 70." Tendulkar was surprised and asked him why would he not average 99? Bradman replied "C'mon, is 70 bad for a 90 year old man?" Bradman was witty, sharp and had a great sense of humour.

The longest partnership of Bradman was with Jessie Menzies. Bradman was 12 and Jessie was 11 when they met for the first time. They got married in 1932 and were together till Jessie passed away in 1997 at the age of 88. Many believed that she was the strength behind Bradman. Jessie's death had a substantial impact on Bradman. He said to people close to him that he had nothing to live for. Bradman followed Jessie to the grave in 2001 at the age of 92.

CHAPTER 2

GOD OF HAPPINESS

Throughout his 24-year career, Sachin Tendulkar dazzled Indian cricket fans with his incredible performance with bat and ball, playing 200 Test matches and 463 One Day Internationals. He will be remembered for his colossal achievements for as long as the game is played. The bat appeared to be an extension of his hand, with an answer to every challenge thrown at him by the best bowlers in the world. And when the ball was tossed to him, he produced streaks of magic that mesmerised even the best batsmen.

Sachin Tendulkar respected the game and played it in good spirits throughout his career, avoiding any controversy - a testament to his impeccable middle-class values. He was aggressive and competitive, but he never crossed the line that would bring the game into disrepute. Because of his strong connection with cricket fans, spectators would throng the stadia before he came out to bat, and many would leave the ground the moment he was out. For many, cricket was Sachin Tendulkar! Despite breaking record after record, he remained humble, and his demeanour was admired by teammates and opponents alike.

Sachin Tendulkar made his debut against a ferocious Pakistan bowling attack that included Wasim Akram, Waqar Younis and Imran Khan when he was 16 years old. India had three consecutive draws when they arrived in Sialkot for the final Test of the Series. Imran Khan had instructed the groundsmen to prepare a green top for the final Test and they had faithfully followed his orders. Tendulkar came in to bat in the second innings with India in a precarious position at 38/4, with an overall lead of 112.

Waqar, who was bowling at the speed of light, got one to bounce a little higher than Tendulkar anticipated and hit him on the nose. When they saw the young lad hit, all the Pakistani players, along with non-striker Navjot Singh Sidhu, ran up to Tendulkar. It was a gruesome scene, with blood oozing from the nose and blood stains on his shirt. Javed Miandad, notorious for his gamesmanship, attempted to scare Tendulkar into believing that his injury was severe and that he should retire hurt and go to the hospital for treatment. Remember, Tendulkar was playing in his first Series, but the heart he displayed by saying "Mein Khelega" ("*I shall play*") was a promise that he was destined for greatness. He went on to score 57 crucial runs and help India save the game.

When asked about the incident many years later, Sachin Tendulkar stated that Coach Ramakant Achrekar would make him bat on difficult pitches and that he had been hurt many times, so he knew what it was like to be hit by a cricket ball. He would raise his pain threshold by tossing the ball into the air and letting it hit his body. These revelations indicated that he was prepared for difficult challenges from an early age.

Tendulkar's visit to the MRF Pace Academy is part of Indian cricket folklore. When Tendulkar was 14, he had a burning desire to become a fast bowler. To develop his fast bowling skills, Tendulkar went to the MRF Pace Academy. He bowled a few balls but failed to impress Dennis Lillee. Seeing Tendulkar standing aside after his trials, Vasu Paranjape, the well-known coach from Mumbai, asked Tendulkar to pad up and bat in the nets. Paranjape had witnessed the young boy's enormous batting ability in school cricket. Tendulkar didn't need a second invitation and was soon stroking the ball beautifully. Seeing Tendulkar's proficiency with the bat, Lillee urged him to focus on batting rather than trying to become a quick bowler. It was possibly the best advice Tendulkar ever received during his entire cricket career. Tendulkar took the advice to heart and went on to become the best batsman of his era. So, while Lillee abruptly ended Tendulkar's dream of becoming a fast bowler, his advice was invaluable to Tendulkar, India, and Cricket.

The incident at the MRF Pace Academy however did not discourage Tendulkar from bowling. Like many batsmen he enjoyed bowling, and his bowling ability was demonstrated in the semi-final of the 1993 Hero Cup. South Africa needed only 6 runs to win in the last over. To bowl that crucial over, Azhar had his regular bowlers Srinath, Kapil Dev and Salil Ankola at his disposal. While the decision on who would bowl the final over was being made, Tendulkar told Azhar that he was confident to bowl the final over. Perhaps Azhar saw Tendulkar as more confident than the other bowlers and decided to bowl him. Interestingly, Tendulkar had not bowled a single ball in the match, and with the chill in the air, his body was stiff, so he took some time to warm up before bowling the first ball. Brian McMillan was on strike and batting brilliantly, so getting him off strike was crucial to India's chances of winning. McMillan smashed the first ball to the cover boundary and set off thinking he could pick up two runs, but as he turned back for the second run, he realised it would be suicidal, so he stopped. But it was too late for non-striker Fanie de Villiers to stop, turn, and return to the crease as Salil Ankola's crisp throw caught him well short of his ground. This brought Allan Donald to the crease, and more importantly, on strike. Donald struggled to get a single, and with each dot ball, the boisterous crowd cheered louder and louder. Clearly, the pressure was mounting on the South African batsmen, while Tendulkar remained calm. Finally, India won a thrilling encounter by 2 runs, thanks to Tendulkar's sensational over. That night, his enthusiasm and ability to contribute as a bowler in a difficult situation stood out. Tendulkar's bowling helped India win numerous matches in the years that followed.

Tendulkar took meticulous care of his equipment, particularly his bat. Even if he got a rough decision, he would not express his displeasure by hurling the bat or gloves around the dressing room. He took great care of his bat and spent hours preparing it for a match. During the process, he began to understand and communicate with the bats. Word spread in the Mumbai Indians' dressing room that Tendulkar has the ability to converse with bats.

Dwayne Bravo, not entirely convinced by this claim, decided to put it to the test. Keiron Pollard joined Bravo as he pulled five cricket bats from his kit bag and asked Tendulkar which bat he should use in the match. Tendulkar got straight to work, flicking the bat with his index finger.

After inspecting all the bats, he ranked them in the order he thought was appropriate.

Bravo then took a bat from another kit bag and told Tendulkar that it was his practice bat and asked how he would rate it. Tendulkar performed the traditional flick with his index finger and stated that this was the bat he should use in the match. Bravo and Pollard were taken aback because they had kept the match bat separate to confuse Tendulkar. However, the bat communicated with him and informed him that it was the best bat. It would not be incorrect to say that bats loved him, obeyed him, and communicated with him; in fact, he had a special relationship with bats.

If Tendulkar talking to cricket bats surprised you, wait until you hear this anecdote. Tendulkar asked Gary Kirsten, the Indian team's coach at the time, to give him a few throw downs because he preferred throw downs to regular net sessions. Kirsten agreed to the throw downs, and the session began.

Every throw down, as usual, found the sweet spot of the bat. After about 15 throw downs, Tendulkar walked up to Kirsten and asked if he noticed anything unusual or if everything was perfectly alright. After a brief pause, Kirsten responded that everything was fine except for Tendulkar's head being slightly raised. Tendulkar then smiled and told Kirsten that he was playing with his eyes closed. Kirsten was taken aback by Tendulkar's ability to play with his eyes closed and wanted to know how he did it. Tendulkar explained to Kirsten that when the hand was raised to release the ball, he would know exactly where the ball would be pitched, allowing him to play with his eyes closed. Kirsten was astounded by Tendulkar's extraordinary talent. Needless to say, only a genius can achieve what mere mortals can only imagine. Tendulkar's enormous success as a batsman comes as no surprise because he picked the line and length early, which is critical to a batsman's success.

Sledging has always existed in cricket, but it has mostly been used by the fielding side to disrupt the batsman's concentration. Tendulkar was sledged during his first tour to Australia, but like most champions, he let his bat do the talking. The word quickly spread in cricket circles that sledging him was a bad idea because it only strengthened his resolve.

Tendulkar was the best batsman in the world by the year 1997. Opposition teams spent the majority of their time in team meetings strategizing how to get rid of him. In general, most teams did not use sledging as part of their strategy to get rid of Tendulkar.

However, this incident took place during the Sahara Cup in Toronto between India and Pakistan. Saqlain Mushtaq made his debut in 1995, and was widely regarded as the world's best off spinner within a few years. His innovative doosra made him a difficult proposition for even good batsmen. Despite having a bag of tricks at his disposal, Saqlain chose sledging to disrupt Tendulkar's concentration. Even though there were no abuses or name-calling, it was an ongoing annoyance, but Tendulkar did not react. He remained silent, concentrating on his batting. After being sledged several times, Tendulkar took Saqlain aside at the end of an over and told him, "You appear to be a good human being, very grounded, and an extremely talented bowler. I have never disrespected you with my words or actions, so why are you sledging me? This was not what I'd expected from you." Tendulkar said this very politely, which embarrassed Saqlain greatly. Saqlain walked away to field near the boundary, but Tendulkar's words rang in his head again and again. For a long time, he couldn't concentrate on the game. Following this incident, Saqlain and Tendulkar clashed on numerous occasions, but Saqlain never said anything; it was purely a battle between the bat and the ball. Their mutual respect grew tremendously over time, and Saqlain, like other opposition players, became a huge fan of Tendulkar.

Here's another intriguing story about Tendulkar's self-confidence. India were chasing 291 runs in an ODI against Australia in Hyderabad and had a terrible start. India were 13-3 when Yuvraj joined the master blaster. However, the duo began cautiously and then opened up. The runs were coming thick and fast, and Australia were beginning to feel the heat.

Ricky Ponting was considering replacing Brad Hogg, who had not been bowling well until the 25th over. Hogg knew he had to do something special, and he did just that. He managed to knock Tendulkar's stumps back on the last ball of the over. Hogg was overjoyed because he had just taken the prize scalp of the world's best batsman. The picture of Tendulkar's dismissal appeared in the next day's newspapers, and Brad Hogg obtained a copy and asked Tendulkar to autograph it for him. Tendulkar agreed and wrote, "Never again mate, ha ha ha. Enjoy the contest. Wish you all the luck!" For the record, Hogg never dismissed Tendulkar in an international match again.

Tendulkar bore the weight of a billion Indian hopes for more than two decades. Every time he took the field, his fans prayed for his success; and when he did, they thought their prayers had been answered. Tendulkar gave every Indian the feeling that he was one of their own; no other cricketer has ever given such an impression. He spread happiness and joy on numerous occasions throughout his career, and the massive fan base he has even after retirement speaks volumes about how he conducted himself on and off the cricket field.

CHAPTER 3

IMPOSSIBLE IS NOTHING

There can be debates about the greatest batsman, bowler and fielder; but there will never be a debate about the greatest all-rounder of all time. Sir Garfield Sobers is undisputedly the greatest all-rounder the game has ever seen. He was a fantastic batsman who was talented and aggressive, as well as an outstanding bowler with excellent control and skill. With his athleticism and grace, he made fielding look so easy, and he took some incredible catches that mere mortals could not have dreamt of catching.

Sobers held two batting world records at one time: the highest individual score by a batsman in a Test innings (365 not out) and the most runs in Test cricket (8032). Brian Lara broke the first record after 36 years when he scored 375 runs, while Geoffrey Boycott broke the latter in 1981.

Initially, Sobers did not set the stage on fire. In fact, he irritated his fans by failing to reach the century mark in his first 22 innings. When he got his first hundred he made it count, scoring 365 not out and breaking Len Hutton's world record by one run. He is still the youngest batsman in history to score a triple century and the first in Test cricket history to convert a maiden ton to a triple century.

While Sobers' world record innings of 365 has become part of the cricketing lore, Don Bradman considers his brilliant innings of 254 to be the best played on Australian soil. The Series between South Africa and Australia was cancelled due to South Africa's global ban on apartheid. In place of the South Africa vs. Australia Series, a Series between the Rest of the World and Australia was organised. Because of the rain, the first Test match ended in a draw. Dennis Lillee, a young tearaway fast bowler from Australia, blew away the Rest of the World in the second Test match at Perth.

The team arrived in Melbourne for the third Test. Lillee once again demonstrated his class by taking 5 wickets and dismissing Sobers for a duck. At the end of the day, Sobers went in to the Australian dressing room, sat beside Ian Chappell and said loudly enough for Lillee to hear, "Ian, you've got a man in here called Lillee, and every time I go in to bat, I seem to be getting these short pitched deliveries, I just want you to tell him that I can bowl short, quick, and bouncers too, so he better watch out for me when he comes in."

As expected, when Lillee came out to bat, Sobers bowled a bouncer that completely unsettled Lillee. Sobers was well aware that a wild shot was just around the corner. The next ball, he pitched it up and took the pace off the delivery, and Lillee had a wild go at it, only to be caught by Bedi at mid-off. At the end of the day, Sobers was back with Ian Chappell in the Australian dressing room. Chappell recalled that earlier in the day, before a fuming Lillee entered the dressing room, the bat hit the wall and he announced that he would continue to bowl more bouncers. To which Sobers calmly replied "He has got the ball and I've got the bat; we'll see."

Lillee greeted Sobers with a barrage of short stuff in the second innings, but was easily dispatched to the boundary. Sobers had not looked menacing in the Series until that innings; then everything changed. And the Sobers the world knew was smashing the balls to the boundary with utter disrespect. Some of the shots were outrageously brilliant, and the spectators were privileged to witness an extremely special innings from an extremely good batsman. None of the Australian bowlers could stop the West Indian southpaw as he smashed his way to a brilliant 254. It was a classic case of 'never taunt a genius or you will pay the price for it.'

The world witnessed the first ever tied Test match during the 1960-61 Series between Australia and the West Indies. Despite the fact that Australia won the Series 2-1, the matches were played in a friendly atmosphere. Gary Sobers had made a name for himself by putting in standout performances against Pakistan, India, and England. A lot was expected of him during his first tour to Australia. West Indies played New South Wales in the lead up to the first Test match in Brisbane. Richie Benaud dismissed Sobers in both innings, prompting the Australian media to claim that Benaud had the wood on Sobers and that the West Indian was unable to pick Benaud's googly. They were confident that Sobers would not pose a threat to Australia.

The teams arrived in Brisbane for the first Test match. Frank Worrell won the toss and chose to bat first without hesitation. Gary Sobers, slotted to bat at No.4, was padded up and nervously sitting outside the dressing room. Seeing the young man tense, Sir Don Bradman walked up to him, tousled his hair and said "Don't you worry son, you'll get it at the right time." Sobers came into bat at the fall of the second wicket and batted for the next three hours, displaying his whole range of strokes and scoring a splendid 132. Richie Benaud was singled out for special treatment by Sobers, putting to rest any questions about his ability to play spin.

In Test cricket, Gary Sobers scored 26 hundreds. However, the last one was very remarkable. It was at Lords in 1973 against England. Sobers was in good form, having hit half centuries in the previous two Test matches; so a big one was not far away. The toss was won by Rohan Kanhai who chose to bat first. Sobers was unbeaten on 31 at the end of the first day's play.

Sobers had never turned down an invitation to go out for a drink, so when Clive Lloyd extended one, he eagerly accepted. They were joined in the night club by some friends, and they all danced and drank until the wee hours of the morning. It was 4am, and Sobers knew that if he went to sleep, he wouldn't wake up in time to bat. So they went back to the hotel and drank until 9am. He then took a cold shower and walked to the ground to get some fresh air!

The first few balls he faced showed signs of a night out. The bat and the ball were going in opposite directions at first, but he soon gathered himself, and the ferocious strokes took over. When he reached 70, he began to experience stomach pain. With the century in sight, he decided to continue the innings. He decided to walk off the ground after completing his century and the pain became unbearable. When he arrived at the dressing room, he told Kanhai that he had stomach pain and that the only medicine he trusted was a shot of port wine and brandy. After gulping down the wine and brandy, Sobers felt much better. Kanhai then asked if he needed another round, to which Sobers replied, "Yes, make it double." He felt good after his second round, so he resumed his innings at the fall of the next wicket. Sobers was unbeaten on 153 runs when Kanhai finally declared the innings. This knock exemplifies Sobers' character of 'Play hard and party hard'!

We all remember Sunil Gavaskar's incredible debut Series against the West Indies in 1971, when he scored 771 runs in four Test matches. But how many of us know that Gary Sobers played a role in his dream debut Series? Gavaskar admits that if it hadn't been for Sobers, he might not have been able to play his second Test match. Gavaskar was on 12 in his first Test match when he played a nervous drive outside the off stump, and the ball went straight to Sobers, who dropped an easy catch. Needless to say, Gavaskar took advantage of the opportunity and scored a half-century, securing his place for the next Test match. In his second Test match, Sobers dropped Gavaskar once again when he slashed a ball outside off stump. Gavaskar was batting on 6. He went on to make a century this time. Gavaskar never looked back and went on to become one of the world's best opening batsmen, tormenting the West Indies with 13 centuries. It was unusual for someone of Sobers' calibre to drop a catch. Gavaskar was fortunate that one of the best fielders in the world dropped him in consecutive Test matches. Gavaskar is certainly correct when he says Sobers opened the gates of cricket for him. Sobers, in a way, gave India a truly fantastic opening batsman.

Gary Sobers could do anything with the bat and the ball. Nobody has or will ever grace the cricket field with the elegance that this genius did for 20 years.

CHAPTER 4

THE COMPLETE CRICKETER

Imran Khan is widely regarded as one of the finest captains in cricket history. That said, his overall talent as a player was remarkable. In his heydays, he possessed the speed, control, and swing to unsettle the best in the game. Initially, his batting was more 'see the ball, hit the ball,' but by the time he hung up his boots, he had developed into an incredibly reliable and confident batsman. Needless to say, his batting average improved significantly. While he was a terrific all-rounder, most people remember him for his astute captaincy, which was the primary reason Pakistan won the World Cup in 1992.

Imran began his bowling career as a tearaway fast bowler, but he quickly realized that control and swing could not be replaced by pace. He was the first bowler in the history of the game who changed his bowling action after playing international cricket, something that was unheard of. Before an injury kept him away from bowling for a few years, he was extremely successful in the early 1980s. Imran played as a batsman during that time and developed his skills, which ultimately helped him in the latter part of his career. Aside from winning the World Cup, he also guided Pakistan to Series victories in India and England. However, he regards the drawn Series against the mighty West Indies in West Indies as the best Series of his career.

Imran had a special ability for seizing every opportunity and gaining the upper hand. For example, he walked out for the toss in a t-shirt with a tiger emblazoned on it for the crucial World Cup match against Australia in Perth in 1992, knowing well that Ian Chappell would question him about the t-shirt. He was correct! After the toss, Chappell asked Imran about the relevance of a tiger on the t-shirt. Imran told Chappell that his team was like caged tigers who had no option but to attack since it was a do-or-die match for Pakistan. Imran had also told the press on the eve of the match that Wasim Akram had been granted a licence to bowl fast and pick up wickets without worrying about wide balls. Imran's statement was printed in big, bold letters in the sports section of all major Australian newspapers. The Australians were rattled by these two incidents, and Pakistan had delivered a decisive blow even before the first ball was bowled.

Imran's exceptional ability to spot talent was one of his many strengths. He was confined to bed one day after contracting food poisoning. With nothing to do, he switched on the television and began watching a match. Imran was leisurely watching the game, but a young bowler bowling with phenomenal speed made him sit up and take notice. The following day, Imran went to the ground and asked the ground staff about the young fast bowler he had loved seeing on television. The ground authorities quickly contacted the young bowler, and as Imran Khan had requested, the young bowler was summoned. Imran handed him a ball and asked him to bowl in the nets. After a few minutes of watching him, Imran informed him that he would be travelling to

Sharjah with the Pakistan squad. The bowler's name was Waqar Younis. Despite his inexperience, Imran recognised a bowler of the highest calibre in him. Waqar mastered the tricks of the trade under Imran's watchful eye and evolved into a terrific bowler who terrorised batsmen all over the world for 15 years.

Imran Khan had a huge impact on Wasim Akram and Waqar Younis. Standing at mid-on or mid-off, Imran would literally tell them what to bowl before every delivery. Waqar, however, once made the decision to think for himself rather than follow Imran's instructions. It happened during the Nehru Cup in India. Pakistan were playing England. The ball was swinging prodigiously, and Waqar was bowling spectacular outswingers. In fact, with 3 slips and 7 fielders on the offside, the field-setting resembled a Test match situation. Waqar would politely inquire after each delivery about whether or not he should get the ball in, but Imran insisted that he bowl only outswingers. After three fruitless tries, Waqar decided to bowl an in-swinger. Big blunder! With no adequate protection on the leg side, the batsman clipped the ball away for a boundary. Imran, who was stationed at mid-on, had to run all the way to the boundary to fetch the ball. Waqar was aware that he was in trouble and hoped that Imran would throw the ball to him, but instead Imran walked up all the way to Waqar and asked if he bowled an inswinger. Waqar, unable to conceal the truth, admitted that he did bowl an inswinger. Imran reacted with the worst of abuses for not following his instructions. Though Imran was immensely supportive of the two W's, he reprimanded them when they went astray. He did everything he could to make them the finest fast bowlers in the world. Both of them admire Imran Khan to this day.

Imran spent a number of years playing County Cricket in England and the Sheffield Shield in Australia. As a result, he was well-versed in the strengths and weaknesses of all the world's major players. Here is an intriguing anecdote recounted by Ramiz Raja that illustrates Imran's observation and evaluation of his opponents. Ramiz was preparing to open the batting in a limited-overs match against New Zealand. Just as he was preparing to leave the dressing room, Imran Khan told Ramiz that he should expect a bouncer from Richard Hadlee in the first few overs. He told him to take an aggressive approach and pull the ball to the boundary, and if he succeeded, Hadlee would not attempt another bouncer in the innings. That's precisely what happened. Hadlee bowled a bouncer at Ramiz in his second over, and it was duly despatched to the boundary. Hadlee did not bowl a single bouncer during the whole innings. Most Pakistani players believe Imran was always one step ahead of the competition and had an uncanny ability to pick the intricate details of his rivals, allowing him to provide the appropriate advice to the players.

Every Pakistani player has a story to share about how Imran's advice improved their performance. During the team meeting a few days before the World Cup Final versus England, Imran agreed to Mushtaq's request to have him bowl when Graeme Hick would come out to bat. Imran, too, believed that Hick was not a good player against spin and would be unable to read Mushtaq's googly. Furthermore, Hick had a very high backlift and would be unable to bring the bat down in time. The moment Hick walked in to bat, Imran brought in Mushtaq as planned. Mushtaq bowled a fast googly that Hick couldn't read, and he was caught in front of the wicket. With the dangerous Hick out of the equation, Pakistan moved a step closer to winning the World Cup. All the players who have played with Imran are emphatic that he would back you completely if you could convince him of anything. Imran had the incredible ability to inspire players to believe in themselves and punch above their weight.

During a visit to Australia in the late 1980s, Imran took a few teammates out to have pizza in a restaurant. Some of the guys had neither been on an overseas tour nor had pizza before. They all ate the pizza that Imran had ordered. When the bill came, Imran took it, calculated his share, put the money on the table, told the others to do the same, and walked away. The teammates were surprised since they expected the captain to pick up the tab, but Imran thought that everyone in the squad was equal and should look after themselves.

Another remarkable incident that proves beyond doubt that Imran never abused his power as captain was when, as the squad was travelling, a player picked up Imran's baggage out of respect, but Imran told him to put it down immediately. He said that both of them were representing Pakistan and that there was no need for him to show respect in this manner.

Imran Khan never considered the possibility of losing while taking tough decisions. That is precisely why he became such a great captain. He possessed a lot of self-confidence and infused it into his team. Imran Khan was a complete package: he was suave, articulate, and a champion all-rounder.

CHAPTER 5

TIGER OF THE CRICKET WORLD

Mansoor Ali Khan Pataudi was the most endearing cricketer of the 1960s and 1970s. Hailing from a royal family, he was suave, stylish, and confident. The flamboyant personality of Pataudi gave the players a feeling of protection. Pataudi, who was educated in England and had previously played for Oxford and Sussex, was unfazed by the white skin. Needless to say, he was a natural leader who took over as captain of the Indian team at the age of 21 after Nari Contractor was hurt in the West Indies by a nasty bouncer from Charlie Griffith. Under his captaincy, India won its first overseas Test match in New Zealand, a testimony to Pataudi's aggressive leadership. Pataudi would have made many appearances in the record books if fate had been kind to him.

Pataudi, nicknamed Tiger, was as graceful and agile as the magnificent beast. His fielding talents were well ahead of his time, and it was thrilling to see him dive and slide in the cover region. Fielding was never taken seriously by Indian players at the time, but Tiger changed that by providing a good example. He put in extra effort and encouraged his sluggish teammates to follow in his footsteps. Indian fielding improved under his leadership. Another notable accomplishment by Pataudi was the development of the spin quartet, and he had such faith in his spinners that he used them in all situations.

Most players who played with Pataudi remember him for his wit and pranks, despite the fact that he was a man of few words. His message was never elaborate, but it was delivered extremely well. Everybody paid attention to what he had to say because it could either be incredibly hilarious or quite serious. He had an aura that even the team's senior players lacked.

The darkest day of Pataudi's life was July 1, 1961. Pataudi was playing for Oxford against Sussex when he and a couple of his teammates went out for dinner at the end of the day's play. After a wonderful Chinese meal, they got into the car provided by wicketkeeper Robin Waters. As they got closer to the hotel, three of Pataudi's teammates decided to walk the remaining distance. They urged Pataudi to join them, but he declined. After his teammates got out of the car, Pataudi sat in the front seat. Just as the car began to pick up speed, another vehicle unexpectedly pulled into the middle of the road. There was no way to avoid a direct collision. When Pataudi struck his right shoulder against the windscreen, he realised that he had severely damaged it. As he was being carried away in the ambulance, he was concerned that he would not be able to participate in the ongoing match. He was advised when he first opened his eyes in the hospital that an urgent procedure was necessary because a glass splinter had entered his eye. The operation was performed, but then on Pataudi had nearly zero vision in the operated eye. It didn't however deter him from doing what he loved: playing cricket. Not long after the horrific incident - in fact just six months later - he made his India debut. It speaks volumes about his immense talent, determination, and courage. Pataudi averaged 34.91 in Test matches when facing fast bowlers with minimal protective gear and one eye.

Sunil Gavaskar recalls a funny incident that took place during the 1966 Moin-ud-Dowla Gold Cup competition when he and Tiger were teammates for the Vazir Sultan Colts Team. On the evening before the game, the players were unsure about how to address Pataudi. So they agreed that whoever contributes to the first wicket should ask Pataudi how he should be addressed. As luck would have it, Gavaskar effected a run out. As the team got together to celebrate the wicket, the other players nudged Gavaskar and reminded him of their conversation the night before. Once he mustered up the courage, Gavaskar asked Pataudi, who was sitting on the ground and tightening his shoelace, in a soft voice, "What should we address you as?" It was then followed by another question: "Should we call you Skipper, Tiger, Pat, or Nawabsaab?" Pataudi stared at Gavaskar, didn't say anything, and went away.

Until the very end, Gavaskar was uncertain as to how to address Pataudi and would never call out to him; instead, if he was a little away from him, he would go up to him!

Ian Chappell recalls Pataudi as a scintillating batsman with a wide range of strokes, epitomised by two superb innings in the Melbourne Test match of the 1967-68 series in Australia. Pataudi was forced to miss the first Test at Adelaide due to a hamstring injury. But since the Indian batting line-up was having trouble, he decided to play in the second Test in Melbourne even though he wasn't fully fit. When Pataudi came in to bat, India were 25 for 5. He had to face the furious Australian attack with one eye and one leg. As if it wasn't enough, the conditions were completely in favour of the bowling side. As a result of the drizzle, the game was repeatedly halted throughout the day. However, nothing stood in the way of Pataudi scoring an enterprising 75 runs in the first innings and an impressive 85 runs in the second innings. During the first innings, Ian Chappell noted that every time play began after a stoppage, Pataudi walked in with a new bat. Chappell, unable to keep his curiosity at bay, enquired about the many bats Pataudi had brought along. Pataudi responded calmly and said that he did not bring any bat on the tour, so he simply picked up the bat closest to the door and walked out to bat. He astonished Chappell even more when he revealed that he only brought one pair of boots, socks, a jacket, a jumper, a pair of trousers, shirts, and abdomen guard for the tour. It obviously indicates that he didn't have his own bats, pads, or gloves, yet he managed to score runs.

Pataudi's pranks were another aspect of him that only those close to him were aware of. While playing in the West Indies, he brought back a dead alligator and placed it on the bed of one of the players. The player came in at 4am and crashed on the bed, not realising there was a dead alligator beside him. Imagine the player's reaction when he woke up the next morning.

Along with Madhavrao Scindia, Pataudi pulled off another remarkable prank when they organised dacoits to abduct Vishwanath. The cricketers had travelled to Gwalior to take part in a match. The car carrying Vishwanath, Chandrashekhar and Prasanna was halted by the dacoits as they were returning through the jungle. Because everything was so expertly orchestrated, Chandrashekhar and Vishwanath were unaware that the entire episode was a set-up. The dacoits sought a large ransom after tying up the players. At first, Vishwanath made an effort to convince the dacoits that India needed their services since they were well-known cricket players. However, the dacoits ignored his plea and told the players that only money could save them. As the dacoits were speaking with Vishwanath, Prasanna attempted to escape since Pataudi had taken him into confidence. As the dacoits pursued Prasanna and fired at him, Prasanna fell into the bushes and fled under the cover of darkness. The dacoits returned and informed Vishwanath that Prasanna had been killed. Vishwanath couldn't keep his emotions in check after learning of his teammate's death. He began to tremble and weep. Pataudi and the others came on the scene when things began to get out of control. The dacoits laid down their guns when they saw Pataudi, but Vishwanath was so terrified that he was not convinced that he had been set free. He was eventually driven to the hotel. Pataudi frequently pulled such pranks on his teammates.

Pataudi lost eyesight in one eye in an unfortunate accident in 1961, but as captain, he had the perfect vision for Indian cricket. After retiring, he remained active in the game, albeit in a limited capacity. The BCCI could have made greater use of his talents since he had an excellent cricket mind. Tiger will undoubtedly be missed by the cricketing world.

CHAPTER 6

THE ORIGINAL MASTER BLASTER

There was an intimidating aura about him every time he walked onto the cricket field, chewing gum. The sight was not one that any of the rival teams enjoyed. He annihilated bowlers, no matter how skilled they were. Because of his apparent high degree of self-confidence, he appeared arrogant. Sir Isaac Vivian Alexander Richards, the first master blaster, captivated audiences all over the world for 17 years. He was referred to as "King" by many of his admirers. With his amazing batting, he truly ruled the cricket world. He was indeed the best batsman by far, and nobody even came close to dethroning him.

Richards did not take a step back when a bowler bowled a bouncer at him, nor did he avoid verbal beamers hurled at him. His excellent responses to the bowlers were fascinating.

In a county match between Somerset and Glamorgan, Greg Thomas the pace bowler from Glamorgan, beat Viv Richards on a couple of occasions. Unable to control his excitement at Richards playing and missing, Thomas walked up to him and in a sarcastic tone said "It's red, round and weighs around 5 ounces." That was a huge blunder by the bowler. It really charged up Richards. The next ball was hammered out of the ground and into a neighbouring river. Richards nonchalantly walked up to Thomas and told him "You know what it looks like; now go fetch it." Not too many bowlers said anything to Richards. And whoever dared to challenge the great man had to eat his words quickly.

Vivian Richards had some fantastic confrontations with some great bowlers on the cricket field. Len Pascoe, though, was the only bowler who attempted to hit him. Along with Dennis Lillee and Jeff Thomson, Pascoe formed a fearsome pace attack that most countries found too hot to handle. Cricketers and commentators of that era believed that he was a very mean bowler. He could bowl in excess of 90mph all day long because he was extremely strong.

There are a few occasions when Pascoe faced off against Vivian Richards. Once, when Pascoe arrived to bowl to Richards, he made it quite clear right away what his objectives were: "The first ball you miss, you're going to the hospital." Vivian Richards turned a deaf ear to the warning. Pascoe bowled 4 bouncers on the trot that Richards just ducked and weaved. Pascoe was unable to hurt Richards, but on the fourth bouncer, as Richards was attempting to evade, his cap fell off. The West Indian picked up the cap, dusted it, and put it on calmly. As he prepared to face the next ball, it was obvious that an explosive delivery was on the way. Richards was well prepared for it and smashed it towards Pascoe. The ball whizzed past Pascoe inches above his head. Richards walked up to Pascoe and said "The hospital guy could have been you."

In an ODI game played in Adelaide, there was yet another Pascoe vs. Richards incident. Pascoe greeted Richards with a bouncer, which Richards attempted to pull but only managed a top edge. The ball flew past the wicketkeeper and sped to the boundary. As was to be expected, the next ball was a bouncer, but Richards had complete control of the shot this time, and the ball sped to the boundary. "That's it, you've bowled your two," the umpire informed Pascoe after he had delivered two bouncers in the over. But, unlike most other batsmen, Richards was not scared of Pascoe's quick and furious bowling. In fact, he didn't have any trouble dealing with fast bowling. "No, let him bowl more," Richards said to the umpire. Of course, Australia's captain, Greg Chappell, stepped in and told Pascoe that if he bowled another bouncer, he would be sent away from the field. That was Vivian Richards; always up for a challenge.

There has been a lot of discussion on how successful Richards would have been if he had to face Roberts, Holding, Garner, Croft, Marshall and the others. But based on what one witnessed in the game between Hampshire and Glamorgan, Richards would have been just as successful against them as he was against Lillee, Thomson, Imran, and other fast bowlers.

Hampshire set a 364-run target for Glamorgan to chase on the final day. While the pitch was flat, Glamorgan did not have an ace team, and Richards was towards the end of his career.

Glamorgan were 140 for 5 at tea on the last day, with Richards at the crease but not at his usual aggressive best. As he had little belief in the Glamorgan batting line-up, Richards was blocking and not making a sincere attempt to chase down the target. Although Hampshire was unsure if they could dismiss Richards, they were confident that the other batsmen wouldn't last the entire session. Richards simply pushed at the first ball after tea, and it raced to the boundary like a bullet. It was the beginning of a spectacular display of outstanding batting, a visual feast for the few thousand spectators on the ground. Richards then seized total control and hammered the Hampshire bowlers into every nook and corner of the ground. The Hampshire players' breath was taken away every time the ball flew away to the boundary. Glamorgan needed 14 runs to win with 3 wickets in hand in the last over of the match. Hampshire captain Mark Nicholas threw the ball to Malcolm Marshall. The strategy was simple: give Richards a single and then finish off the three wickets.

Two of the greatest players to play the game and also teammates of the greatest team ever, were now facing off. Marshall roared in and bowled a length ball that was dismissed with disdain to the cover boundary. The equation read 10 runs needed to win off 5 balls. Mark Nicholas asked Marshall to give a single and have a go at the other batsman. Marshall steamed in again and bowled a bouncer. Richards went forward but quickly rocked back and pulled it over square leg for a mighty six. Now four runs were required off four balls. Mark Nicholas screamed to Marshall from long-off to give Richards a single. As Marshall sprinted in again, everyone waited with bated breath for the outcome of the third delivery. But Richards took their breath away with a spectacular shot. It was a full-length delivery, but Richards was up to it. He dug the ball out and it sped off to the long-on boundary in a jiffy. Richards had single-handedly pulled off an unbelievable victory. There was no doubt that it was a top-quality performance by a top-level batsman. As the players raced back to the dressing rooms, Richards extended his hand to Mark Nicholas and remarked, "That was one helluva declaration, skipper; let's go drink some beers."

Imran Khan paid the ultimate tribute to Vivian Richards. He said that most batsmen would not relish facing fast bowlers, especially those with extra pace, which would give the fast bowlers the edge. But this was not the case with Richards. Since Richards had exceptional eyesight he picked the ball early and always opted for the aggressive approach. Imran concluded by saying that it was a harrowing experience bowling to the master blaster who was head and shoulders above the rest.

CHAPTER 7

GEM FROM THE EMERALD ISLAND

Arjuna Ranatunga appeared to be anything but a sportsman, even during his playing days. His midriff was ample proof that fitness was not his top priority. While Ranatunga was not the fastest on the field, no one's brain worked faster than his in the 1990s. He was astute, opportunistic, and well-versed with the rules of the game, which made him an extremely confident and inspiring leader. In fact, Arjuna Ranatunga was responsible for the rise of Sri Lankan cricket in the 1990s and the subsequent World Cup victory.

Ranatunga did not shy away from an argument and never backed down. In fact, his detractors thought he went looking for one at times. His ability to handle pressure was a quality that made him a natural leader. When Muralitharan was called for chucking during the tour of Australia, Ranatunga backed him to the hilt. As a mark of protest he stopped the game. But while leaving the playing field, he made sure that the rest of the team remained on the ground. Ranatuga was well aware that if the entire team left the ground, the match would be forfeited. The umpires would then be within their rights to award the match to Australia. Ranatunga's distinctive style of protest earned sympathy for Sri Lanka from the entire cricket world.

Ranatunga was inspired by two captains from the subcontinent, Kapil Dev and Imran Khan - both of whom had won World Cups. Ranatunga began the preparations eighteen months before the World Cup. He carefully selected his team, picking only those who believed they could win the Championship. Any player who questioned the team's ability was not considered for selection.

Aravinda de Silva was the vice captain and the batting anchor for Sri Lanka. Ranatunga recognised Aravinda's value in the squad since their batting revolved around him. There is an interesting anecdote that shows how far Ranatunga went to keep Aravinda happy. In Australia, a bus ride would take up to two hours. Aravinda was the only member of the team who listened to English music. The rest of the squad was into Sinhalese music. Ranatunga could not upset his team or his deputy. So he persuaded everyone in the squad except Aravinda to chip in and buy a Walkman. He then gave it to Aravinda and told him to listen to whatever music he wanted while the rest of the players listened to Sinhalese music. Ranatunga went to great lengths to ensure that Aravinda was always in a good frame of mind. And Aravinda vindicated his captain's confidence in him by batting beautifully in the World Cup semi-final and final.

Arjuna Ranatunga's exceptional captaincy is exemplified by the two incidences that occurred just before the World Cup final.

After defeating India in the semi-final at Kolkata, Ranatunga and his team boarded a flight to Lahore for the final against Australia. Two Indian journalists who were friends with Ranatunga visited him in his hotel room. During the talk, they told him to go after the Aussies at the news conference before the final. Ranatunga gladly agreed, seeing the opportunity to start the battle before the teams met in the final.

Around 300 journalists were present at the press conference, waiting impatiently for Ranatunga to give the headline for their publications. The decision as to which journalist could pose a question rested with the gentleman in the hot seat. When Ranatunga arrived, he had a look around. His journalist buddies were both sitting, one at either end of the room.

As soon as the press conference began, Ranatunga went straight to one of his journalist friends, "What's your question?" The journalist asked, "What do you think of Shane Warne?" Ranatunga unhesitatingly replied, "Shane Warne is highly overrated; in fact he is a mediocre bowler." The journalist asked him a follow up question, "Do you think he is a match winner?" Ranatunga dismissed it by declaring, "He is not a match winner when he plays against us." After replying to another question, he went to the other journalist who asked him, "What do you think of the Waugh brothers?" Ranatunga with a straight face answered, "They, too, are mediocre players, and there are many better players in Asia, but our media ignores them."

The journalists were so delighted with the spice that they published the full interview word for word in the next day's newspapers. The battle had begun even before the toss. Obviously, the Australians were caught off guard. It was the first time they had to respond to the rival captain's comments. The effect was evident as Sri Lanka easily defeated Australia in the final.

Another instance of Ranatunga's astute cricket judgement was asking Australia to bat first in the final. In every prior final, the team that set the score won. However, Ranatunga's choice to field first was based on information he gathered a couple of nights before the final.

The Australians had completed net practice and had left the ground. While the Sri Lankans were practising under lights, Ranatunga noticed a significant dew cover. He asked the groundsman whether such heavy dew was normal. The groundsman answered in the affirmative. On the eve of the final, there was a dinner hosted for both the teams. After dinner, when everyone was retiring to their individual rooms, Ranatunga and manager Duleep Mendis drove to the ground to confirm the dew. As expected, there was a thick cover of dew on the ground.

When Ranatunga was coming out for the toss, Imran Khan, the local boy of Lahore, asked him what he would do if he won the toss. Without revealing his thoughts, Ranatunga asked Imran what he would have done. Imran said that he would bat first because it was the final, and scoreboard pressure would be significant. Not wishing to disregard the thought, he went to Duleep Mendis and informed him about his conversation with Imran. Overhearing the discussion, Arvinda de Silva insisted on Sri Lanka batting first. However, Duleep Mendis and Arjuna Ranatunga had already decided to chase. And they were confident that dew would definitely set in, during the second innings.

When the Australians came out to defend the score, the dew made it difficult for the spinners, including Shane

Warne, to grip the ball. Sri Lanka won by 7 wickets, with Ranatunga hitting the winning runs.

Ranatunga was one of the finest captains of his day; although his contribution to the team as a batsman is hardly mentioned. Ranatunga was not the fittest and would save energy by walking across the pitch when taking singles, but when the necessity arose, he was pretty quick. He used his brain while batting, just as he did as captain. He would choose the right bowler to go after, and it would come off.

Graeme Smith and Malcolm Marshall have both been applauded as batsmen who came to bat with a broken finger and hand. However, nothing is spoken about Ranatunga's bravery in batting with a fractured finger and leading his side to victory.

Sri Lanka were chasing 220 to win an ODI against Pakistan, and were 146 for four when Ranatunga was struck on the thumb by Waqar. He was in agony and had to leave the field with a fractured finger.

Following Ranatunga's departure, Pakistani spinners began to make serious inroads into Sri Lanka's batting order, and the scoreboard soon read 177 for 8. At the time, it appeared like Pakistan would easily win the contest. Against all odds, Ranatunga emerged from the pavilion to support Romesh Kaluwitharana. Ranatunga knew batting would be difficult since he couldn't grip the bat with his bottom hand. Most of the time, he would use one hand to keep the ball away from the stumps, and on other occasions, he would use the pace of the bowler to play it behind the wicket for runs.

It was a brilliant example of mind over matter, and even though he was in excruciating pain, his determination to succeed was paramount in his mind. As runs began to trickle in, Sri Lanka was getting closer to the target. With each run, Pakistan's bowlers and fielders came under intense pressure, and the batsmen's confidence was growing. The partnership might have been broken a few times, but for the poor fielding effort of the Pakistanis. It was hard to say whether Pakistan's fielding or the running between the wickets by the Sri Lankan batsmen was worse.

After some close calls, Ranatunga against the run of play hit a boundary on the offside. The Sri Lankan camp rejoiced as that boundary alleviated pressure. Finally, Kaluwitharana smashed two successive boundaries to take Sri Lanka home. It was a thrilling game in which Sri Lanka snatched victory from the jaws of defeat.

Sri Lanka has had some outstanding players and captains over the years, but none can match the brilliance of the portly Arjuna Ranatunga.

CHAPTER 8

LORD OF LORDS

Dilip Vengsarkar initially showed signs of greatness in the winter of 1975 at Nagpur, against an experienced Rest of India bowling attack. Walking in to bat with Mumbai at 98 for 3, Vengsarkar produced a superb century on a track that was spinning square, and against spinners who lured batsmen to their doom all over the world. He hammered Bedi and Prasanna into the stands with incredible ease. Vengsarkar's fluent stroke play astounded everyone. One of them was the legendary Lala Amarnath, who saw a striking resemblance between Vengsarkar's big hitting and that of Col C. K. Naydu. That's how Vengsarkar got the nickname Colonel. He never batted with so much aggression again after that spectacular innings.

After his blitzkrieg innings in Nagpur, it was just a matter of time before Vengsarkar made it to the Indian team. During India's tour of New Zealand in 1975-76, he earned his first Test cap. Interestingly, he opened the innings. Although India won, Vengsarkar did not taste success. Not long after his poor performance as an opener, he dropped down the order and began batting at No. 3 and No. 4 for India. Between 1983 and 1987, he was widely regarded as the finest batsman in the world.

Vengsarkar holds the distinction of becoming the only non-English batsman to score three centuries at Lords.

He fondly recalls the third century he scored at the home of cricket in 1986. When the last man, Maninder Singh, arrived at the crease, Vengsarkar was on 85. He warned Maninder that if he got out playing a reckless shot, he would not return home. Maninder had denied Vengsarkar a century in Sri Lanka by playing a terrible shot and getting out, leaving Vengsarkar stranded on 98. However, this time Maninder did not let Vengsarkar down and remained with him till he hit a century and made it into the record books. Even to this day, Vengsarkar's elegant stance enriches the majestic wall at Lords.

While he took immense pride in playing for India, it did not dwindle even a bit when he represented Bombay. Every time he took the field for Bombay, he played with the same energy and intensity. He played a wonderful captain's innings in one of the all-time great Ranji Trophy matches, but unfortunately ended up on the losing side after scoring 139 not out.

The Ranji Trophy final between Bombay and Haryana was played in the sweltering heat of Bombay in May 1991. Bombay were obviously the favourites, while Haryana were the underdogs. Furthermore, the final was held in Wankhede stadium, giving Bombay a significant advantage. The contest was a star-studded affair. Both teams boasted of international stars, albeit Bombay had more star power than Haryana. Bombay's line-up included Vengsarkar, Tendulkar, Manjrekar, Pandit, Rajput, Kambli, Raju Kulkarni, and Salil Ankola, while Haryana's line-up included Kapil Dev and Chetan Sharma.

Haryana took a decisive first-innings lead. Mumbai needed 355 runs on the last day to win in just over two sessions. Unfortunately, they got off to a bad start and went to lunch at 34 for 3. After lunch, Tendulkar and his skipper, Vengsarkar, forged an excellent partnership. Just when Bombay seemed to be taking control of the game, Tendulkar got out. Then, Kambli and Vengsarkar formed a good partnership, but after Kambli's departure, wickets began to tumble.

As the ninth wicket fell at 305, Bombay needed 50 runs to win. Vengsarkar then blasted Yogesh Bhandari for 26 runs in an over, and Bombay were suddenly within striking distance of an improbable victory. But, sadly, there was a twist in the tale. Kuruvilla was run out and Bombay lost by two runs. Vengsarkar found it incredibly difficult to accept the loss. He slumped to the ground and started sobbing. Even when he returned to the dressing room, he was weeping. Sanjay Manjrekar, who played a lot of cricket with Vengsarkar, says that he had never seen him weep before. According to Vengsarkar, he was unable to sleep for three months due to the defeat.

After many years, Vengsarkar recalled a fascinating conversation he had with Kapil Dev during the tea break. Kapil requested Vengsarkar that he should allow Haryana to win at least once. Vengsarkar said that Haryana was in control and that victory was inevitable. In response, Kapil stated that he was not certain of winning as long as Vengsarkar was around. Kapil had played enough cricket with Vengsarkar to know the immense potential of the Bombay captain.

One of the fiercest rivalries in the game was between Dilip Vengsarkar and Malcolm Marshall. The seeds were sown during the 1978-1979 West Indies tour of India. Marshall was a total novice who was still learning the tricks of the trade. When Vengsarkar claimed a bat-pad catch while fielding at silly point, the umpire upheld the appeal. Marshall was unhappy because he thought he wasn't out. Throughout his career, he bowled aggressively every time he encountered Vengsarkar at the crease. In the 1983 World Cup group game, Marshall injured Vengsarkar, preventing him from playing the remainder of the tournament.

For something he believed in, Vengsarkar was willing to stand his ground. The personality of Vengsarkar is reflected by a highly intriguing incident that took place in 1982. A match between Sunil Gavaskar XI and Intikhab Alam XI was organised in Sharjah by Asif Iqbal, a former Pakistani cricketer, and Abdul Rahman Bukhatir, the head of UAE cricket. Even though Sharjah was yet to stage an international cricket match, it was on its way to becoming one.

The Indian squad and a few Bollywood celebrities were on board the flight when it arrived in Sharjah. All cricket fans who grew up watching the sport in the 1980s and 1990s will agree there was always a strong presence of Bollywood celebrities at the stadium. They unquestionably brought glitz and glamour to the gruelling cricket matches.

As the cricketers and movie stars waited in line for customs clearance, the customs officer called the movie stars. Cricketers were not treated on par with movie stars at the time. Needless to say, the cricketers made no protests.

But Dilip Vengsarkar was unwilling to tolerate the customs officer's behaviour and expressed his unhappiness in Marathi, which the officer took offence to. Unfortunately, the obstinate officer refused Vengsarkar entry into the UAE on that trip. As a result, he was sent home. The Mumbai star was displeased with the treatment he received, but he was even more outraged that none of his colleagues supported him, including the captain Sunil Gavaskar. According to speculations, this episode strained the relationship between the two Mumbai cricketing heavyweights.

On tours, Dilip Vengsarkar, Sanjay Manjrekar and Sachin Tendulkar frequently hung out together even though they were not all of the same age. Despite his seniority and experience, Vengsarkar felt at ease with the two young cricketers from his hometown.

In 1990, Dilip Vengsarkar was involved in a funny incident that took place in New Zealand. The Indian team was lodging in a stunning resort in a serene and peaceful environment. There were trees all around the magnificent property. Tendulkar and Manjrekar were roommates, since back then players shared rooms. As a senior player, Vengsarkar was offered a single room, but he preferred to share it with another player because he was scared to be alone at night. Knowing this, the two young Mumbaikars planned to create a frightening tale to scare Vengsarkar one evening when they were strolling after dinner.

Manjrekar innocently asked Tendulkar to elucidate on the white saree woman he saw on a tree at the Sahitya Sahawas colony, which was Tendulkar's home at the time. Tendulkar picked the cue immediately and started making up a story. With every passing minute, it was evident that Vengsarkar was feeling nervous. He eventually discovered that his two young colleagues were merely attempting to scare him. He referred to them as brats and went to his room.

There was a knock on the door after around 10 minutes. When Manjrekar opened the door, he was surprised to see Dilip Vengsarkar. In no uncertain terms, Vengsarkar declared that he too would sleep in the same room with Manjrekar and Tendulkar. The story had the intended impact. Dilip Vengsarkar had no fear of facing the world's quickest bowlers, but he found it difficult to sleep alone at night.

Given that he has scored four centuries in the Indian capital, he is entitled to the title 'King of Kotla'. But smashing three centuries at the mecca of cricket is truly remarkable, so there can't be a better title for Dilip Vengsarkar than 'Lord of Lords'.

Chapter 9

The Cricketer who Loved a Fight

Over the years, Pakistan has produced some great batsmen like Zaheer Abbas, Majid Khan, Inzamam-ul-Haq, Asif Iqbal, Mohammed Yousuf etc, but there was daylight between Javed Miandad and the rest of them. Miandad was an entertainer and there was never a dull moment while he was batting or fielding. He was skillful, courageous, and had a remarkable cricket brain.

Javed Miandad, along with Imran Khan, was the backbone of Pakistan cricket from the early 1980s until the 1990s. Imran has stated that whenever Pakistan needed someone to stand up and score runs in challenging situations, Miandad would invariably take charge. Imran and Miandad were like chalk and cheese, yet they kept their disagreements aside for the benefit of Pakistan cricket.

After Pakistan was defeated by India in 1979, Asif Iqbal's captaincy was revoked, and Miandad was appointed captain at the age of 22. Surprisingly, he was chosen over experienced players like Majid Khan, Sarfraz Nawaz, Wasim Bari, and Zaheer Abbas. The senior players were unhappy with his selection as captain. And after a couple of years the opposition grew stronger, and Miandad lost his captaincy despite his 'not-too-bad' performance.

Javed Miandad's incredible self-belief was obvious long before he earned a reputation for himself in international cricket. His team needed 18 runs in 3 balls in a club match. Miandad convinced his coach to let him bat since he was sure to hit 3 sixes. The team's captain was the batsman on strike, but after seeing Miandad's confidence, the coach asked him to retire hurt and return to the dressing room. Miandad strode to the crease and smashed the next 3 balls for 3 magnificent sixes winning the match for his club.

All through his career, he was unfazed by any challenge or situation. In the early 1970s, Pakistan's first cricket captain, Abdul Hafeez Kardar, a prominent administrator, said that Javed Miandad was the player of the decade after watching him play. And he was dead right. Miandad struck a century and a double century in his first and third Test against New Zealand. Needless to say, there was no looking back after his debut Series.

Javed Miandad was so passionate about cricket that he was prepared to play for Pakistan even after retirement. There's an amazing story about Miandad's intense desire to play even after hanging up his boots. Miandad had travelled to New Zealand with the Pakistani squad as their coach. Unfortunately, some of the team's frontline batsmen suffered injuries. After a net session, captain Inzamam-ul-Haq was in the dressing room, contemplating how to find replacements before the next Test match. It was challenging back then to quickly fly a player from Pakistan to New Zealand. When Miandad saw Inzamam, he approached him and informed him that he had found a batsman in New Zealand who could join the squad. Inzamam was really interested in who the batsman was while having a clear expression of doubt. Miandad then stated emphatically that the batsman was none other than himself. Not wishing to turn down Miandad's offer, Inzamam informed him that he had not had a net session since retirement, making it impossible for him to bat against international bowlers. Miandad promptly told him that he would go out for a net session and prepare for the upcoming Test match. With a lot of difficulty, Inzamam convinced Miandad that it was not a good idea. And his offer to play was turned down.

Javed Miandad's grasp of the game was truly extraordinary. Here's a glimpse of Javed Miandad's cricket brain at work. Pakistan was playing Sri Lanka in a Test Series. During one of the net sessions, Inzamam told Miandad that he was having trouble with Muralitharan's off spin. Miandad took a pause before advising Inzamam that driving Muralitharan through the covers was the best way to play his off spin. A perplexed Inzamam tried to convince Miandad that just surviving was difficult, leave alone driving against the spin. After the net session, Miandad told Inzamam to bat at the end from where the bowlers had bowled. The spike marks had obviously created a rough, so batting would be difficult. Miandad then began throwing the ball into the rough. Because of the uneven surface, some balls spun, some stayed low, and others jumped dangerously. Initially, Inzamam struggled to put bat to ball, but he gradually began driving, and by the end of the practice session, he was confident about playing Muralitharan. The following day, as soon as Muralitharan began his spell, Inzamam repeatedly drove him through the covers. Muralitharan immediately changed the line from outside the off stump to middle and leg. Batting became relatively easy as Inzamam started to pick up singles on the leg side with the turn. The threat was averted, and Inzamam never had any issues dealing with Muralitharan. It is fair to presume that Javed Miandad was one of the few cricketers in the world who truly mastered the art of batting.

Contrary to popular belief, it was Javed Miandad, not Imran Khan, who spotted and selected Wasim Akram to play Test cricket. The narrative of how Akram made it to the Pakistan Test team is fascinating. A summer camp was organised at the Gaddafi stadium in Lahore. Many young bowlers were present to demonstrate their abilities. The tall, lanky, and inexperienced Wasim Akram was one of them. Wasim Akram had the good fortune to bowl to Pakistan's Test captain Miandad, who had gone to the Gaddafi Stadium for a net session. When Akram was asked to bowl to the legendary Miandad, he admits he was nervous. After facing a few deliveries from Akram, Miandad was convinced of the left-arm fast bowler's enormous potential. The difficulty now was to get him in the team, and as predicted, the selection panel was resistant. Miandad had no option but to use his connection with the PCB's President, Lt. Gen. Ghulam Butt, to forward Akram's case. Miandad convinced the President of PCB, and Akram boarded the flight to New Zealand. After Akram took 10 wickets in his second Test match, there was no looking back. Who knows? Without Miandad, Akram may never have played for Pakistan.

Here's yet another illustration of Miandad's smart cricket brain and his capability to quickly adjust to various circumstances. Before the 1996 World Cup, a camp was organised, and it was every youngster's dream to play in the World Cup. Young Saqlain Mushtaq, who made his debut for Pakistan in 1995, was keen to be a part of the World Cup team. Javed Miandad was also in the camp and hoped to cap off his magnificent career by winning the World Cup. Saqlain's doosra and off spin caught Miandad off guard in every net session. But every time he got out, Miandad would smile and tell Saqlain that he has a different plan for the match. Saqlain felt that Miandad was trying to manipulate him by downplaying the dismissals.

A practice game was organised between two teams, one captained by Ramiz Raja and the other by Wasim Akram. Saqlain and Miandad were in opposing teams. As luck would have it, Saqlain was the bowler when Miandad walked in to bat. As soon as he arrived at the crease, Miandad told Saqlain to forget about the net sessions and focus on the game instead, since he would use a new batting approach. Miandad took guard, looked around the field, and changed his batting stance. It perplexed Saqlain, who had been confident up to that point and had planned to attack Miandad with a ring of fielders. Saqlain thought of altering the field for a moment before dismissing the idea. The first ball was on the off stump, and Miandad got into position with a couple of quick foot movements and blasted the ball to the boundary on the offside. Saqlain had never seen Miandad move his feet in the nets in this manner. The new approach by Miandad baffled Saqlain to the extent that he once again considered moving the field, but Ramiz assured him that the field placement was fine and that he would get Miandad out. On the second ball, Saqlain decided not to give Miandad any room and bowled the ball on the middle and leg stump. Miandad picked the paddle sweep from his extensive repertoire of strokes. There was no protection in the fine-leg region, so the ball raced away to the boundary. Saqlain's confidence was shaken after two boundaries in two balls, so he decided to allow Miandad a single and keep him off the strike. As the next ball left Saqlain's hand, Miandad came down the wicket and hammered him for a six. 14 runs in three balls! At the end of the over, Miandad went up to Saqlain and asked him whether he saw a difference in his batting. Saqlain responded by simply bowing respectfully to Miandad's extraordinary talent.

Javed Miandad played with the opponent's psyche. He was always one step ahead of the game and never missed an opportunity. Miandad is one of just two batsmen in Test cricket (the other being Herbert Sutcliffe of England) whose average never fell below 50. And this reflects his incredible consistency. Without a question, Javed Miandad was a fighter who never gave up; in fact, he cherished and welcomed difficult situations.

Chapter 10

The Voice of Cricket

Anthony William Greig, better known as Tony Greig, had a truly international connection with the game of cricket. He was born in South Africa, played for England, loved Sri Lanka, and eventually made Australia his home.

Greig was 6.6 feet tall and had a towering personality that few could match. For many who began watching cricket in the 1990s, Tony Greig was the epitome of cricket commentary, bringing tremendous excitement with his distinct voice and impeccable style. Many people forget that Tony Greig was one of the world's best all-rounders in the 1970s. He wasn't the most technically sound batsman, but he overcame his flaws with grit and determination. He was not a fast bowler, but that did not stop him from taking on the finest batsman in the world. Greig was always up for a challenge and never backed down.

Despite being a highly conservative left-wing politician, Greig's father let him choose cricket over university studies. Greig received a contract offer from Sussex, and in his debut game there, he smashed a superb century against Lancashire, who had a very potent bowling attack. It opened the door to a wonderful career. In 1972, he made his England debut. A few years later, he was named England captain.

When Greig walked in to bat in his debut match against Lancashire, Umpire Dusty Rhodes asked Brian Statham about the young batsman who had just walked in. Statham told the umpire that it was Greig from South Africa.

The first ball Greig faced from Statham struck him on the pads in front of the wicket. But to everyone's surprise, including Greig's, the umpire rejected the appeal. Greig took a single of the next ball and went to the non-striker's end. Umpire Rhodes gently enquired "By any chance are you related to Sandy Greig?" "He is my father," said Tony Greig. Umpire Rhodes looked down the wicket and said "Great decision!"

In fact, while Umpire Rhodes was a cricket coach in South Africa about 20 years before Greig made his debut for Sussex, he and Greig's father would meet for a drink every evening. Greig believed that in life such lucky breaks lead you to success. If the umpire had ruled him out when he was on zero, he might not have made the playing eleven for the next match. Umpire Rhodes's favourable decision enabled Greig to score a superb 156, and the rest, as they say, is history.

During his playing days, Greig flirted with controversy time and again. He got severely criticized for running out Alvin Kalicharan in Port-of-Spain, though till his last breath Greig believed that he had done nothing wrong.

It was the last ball of the day. Bernard Julien was the batsman, while Kalicharan was at the non-striker's end on 142. Greig was fielding at silly point. Julien hit the last ball of the day a couple of metres to the right of Greig, who reached the ball in two steps and scooped up only to find Kalicharan outside the crease and walking towards the pavilion. The ball was in play according to the rules of the game since the umpire had not called "Stumps!" Greig instinctively threw the ball at the stumps and appealed. The umpire gave him out. Kalicharan got enraged and smashed the bat on the ground. The audience went wild when they saw an angry Kalicharan. Some English players believed that if the incident had happened in Guyana or Jamaica, the scenario would have been far more dangerous because the crowds on those islands were much more hostile.

The English team's manager and captain were asked to stay back for a discussion. After hours of deliberation between West Indies board members, captain Mike Denness, and manager Donald Carr, it was decided that England would withdraw the appeal and Kalicharan would continue to bat. When play resumed the following day, Greig was asked by manager Donald Carr to shake hands with Alvin Kalicharan on the field. He resisted the request but eventually consented. Greig's competitive nature and enthusiasm led him to act in a manner that placed his sportsmanship under question, but it did not alter the way he approached the game.

Throughout his career, he was never intimidated by the antagonistic pace of Australian or West Indian bowlers. He and Dennis Lillee got into an altercation at Brisbane during the opening Test of the 1974 Ashes Series. Greig used the bouncers generously when Lillee came to bat, which angered the Australian. As soon as Lillee was dismissed by a bouncer, he said to Greig, "Remember you started it." The battle lines were drawn! Thomson and Lillee bowled with fire, but Greig held his own and slammed a spectacular century in the first innings. Every time he hit a four, he teased Lillee by signalling a boundary. That was Tony Greig for you. Cheeky and eager for a confrontation, regardless of the opponent. Perhaps it was his South African upbringing that encouraged him to play cricket in a manner that few would dare.

Tony Greig led England against the West Indies in 1976. The West Indies were soundly beaten by the Australians and very narrowly defeated India at home. However, there was no denying that they were a bunch of incredibly talented cricketers. They had begun to attract a lot of attention from fans and the media. During one of the media interviews, Greig uttered the most infamous line in cricket history: "We will make them grovel." Coming from an English captain of South African origin during the apartheid era, the ramification increased significantly. The West Indies bowlers became more determined as a result, and they began to bowl exceptionally quick, making it dangerous for the English batsmen to play.

Every time Greig came in to bat, the bowlers added a yard of pace and upped the number of bouncers to a minimum of three in an over. They would limit the number of bouncers after Greig was dismissed. Dennis Amiss even jokingly said that he wished for Greig to be dismissed so that it would calm the West Indies bowlers and make batting relatively easy. At the conclusion of the penultimate day of the Series, with West Indies certain to win, Greig made his way into the open stands, which were largely populated by West Indies fans. There, he knelt down and crawled a short distance. Greig used it as a way of making amends for using the word "grovel".

There was mutual admiration between Tony Greig and the Indian crowd. They appreciated the antics of Greig. During the 1973 tour to India, in the Test match at the Brabourne stadium, Greig won the hearts of the Indian public with an act that is etched in the minds of every Indian cricket fan. When Vishwanath scored a brilliant hundred, Greig spontaneously picked and cradled Vishwanath with a packed stadium cheering on. It was a beautiful sight that revealed Greig's gentler side.

Greig realized that his playing days were numbered and wanted financial security. So when Kerry Packer offered him a contract for World Series Cricket he readily agreed. He also managed to secure a lifelong deal as a commentator with Channel 9. Greig acted as an agent for Packer in recruiting players from around the world. With the introduction of the white ball and coloured clothing, big money flowed in. Greig's contribution to the World Series Cricket was not appreciated by the English Board, and as a result he lost his captaincy and was later dropped from the team.

The World Series Cricket lasted from 1977 to 1979, when the Australian Board and Kerry Packer agreed to a truce. Greig decided it was time to move from being a player to a commentator, and so his second innings began by dropping the bat and picking up the microphone. His exuberant commentary was unconventional and unique, making him an immediate favourite with the audience. Tony Greig, along with Richie Benaud, Bill Lawry and Ian

Chappell, formed the fantastic four in the commentary box. Each of the four commentators brought something distinctive to the table, elevating broadcasting to a new level.

33 years after starting to commentate for Channel 9, Greig missed the opening Test match at the Gabba for the very first time as he was fighting lung cancer. For years, Greig had made it a morning ritual to drive Richie Benaud and Ian Chappell to the ground, and this was the first time Greig wasn't present. From the hotel foyer, Ian Chappell promptly made a call to Greig to inform him that they were waiting for him downstairs. Greig, who was resting at home, chuckled through his pain and said "See you soon."

Greig was also diagnosed with epilepsy at the age of 14, but never let the condition interfere with his passion for the game. He controlled epilepsy so successfully with the help of his teammates and appropriate medicine that many people didn't even realise he had it for a long time. Sadly, he is no longer with us; the cricket world will miss him.

Chapter 11

The Gentle Giant

During the 1992 World Cup, the world first heard about this exceptionally talented batsman named Inzamam-ul-Haq. He handled the willow with such lazy elegance that everybody who watched him bat gasped in admiration. Although a lot of people credit Imran Khan with finding Inzamam, Wasim Raja (Ramiz Raja's brother) actually had a far greater role in identifying the potential of this batting sensation from Multan.

Pakistan had just returned from a closely fought Series in the West Indies, and Ramiz was brimming with confidence after a successful tour. One night at the dinner table, Wasim Raja told Ramiz that Inzamam ought to have been a part of the West Indies tour. Obviously, Inzamam had impressed Wasim Raja, who had taken a Pakistan U-19 squad to Australia. Ramiz had apparently never heard of Inzamam; so he gently inquired whether Inzamam was a fast bowler, since Pakistan had a tradition of inducting fast bowlers at an early age. Wasim Raja surprised Ramiz by telling him that Inzamam was a batsman and not a bowler. Within Pakistani cricket circles, word quickly spread about Inzamam's remarkable talent.

One day, Inzamam received an invitation to the Gadaffi Stadium. When he arrived, Imran Khan and Mudassar Nazar were present, and he was instructed to bat on the centre wicket. Not only that, but he had to deal with Waqar, Aaqib, Mohsin Kamal and Mushtaq Ahmed. Under fading light, the new ball was given to the fast bowlers. Inzamam was nervous, and it was evident in the way he played the first few balls. In fact, he was out a few times, but Waqar and Mushtaq, with whom he had played a lot of cricket and who were also his close friends, gave him the confidence that he was too good a player to get out.

When it appeared that Inzamam was getting intimidated by the occasion, Mohsin Kamal dropped a ball short. It was just what Inzamam needed to get his game back on track. He pulled the ball a long way. The pull shot gave him a lot of confidence. Inzamam had found his stride, and what followed was pure slaughter. He seemed to have no trouble with any of them as he thrashed every bowler with ease. At the end of the session, an overjoyed Imran Khan told Mudassar Nazar that Pakistan had found its Vivian Richards. Imran Khan recognised Inzamam's worth on Australia's quick, bouncy tracks after observing his ability to play short balls and took the decision to select him for the 1992 World Cup team.

At the beginning of the World Cup, Inzamam struggled and fell short of his captain's expectations but Imran Khan was unconcerned. However, when Inzamam was struggling in the early rounds of the World Cup, a senior Pakistani player told him he was no good and that he should not have been selected for the World Cup. Inzamam was deeply hurt by this humiliation, and he sobbed for half an hour in the shower. Imran Khan, on the other hand, was a great fan of Inzamam. Throughout the World Cup, Imran stated two things: Pakistan will win the World Cup, and Inzamam would win it for them. In the end both came true. In order to avoid exposing the young man to face the new ball, Imran actually pushed Inzamam down to No. 6 and elevated himself to No. 3. It was a master stroke!

Pakistan needed to beat New Zealand in the World Cup's final group match to proceed to the semi-final. Inzamam failed yet again, but this time, just before he was dismissed, he unleashed a ferocious pull shot that sent the ball racing towards the boundary. As a result of Pakistan's triumph, the squad was required to fly from Christchurch to Auckland to play in the semi-final. Inzamam was depressed since he had yet to deliver at the World Cup. Even worse, he had a seat on the aircraft right next to Imran Khan. Inzamam was terrified, convinced that Imran would reprimand him. Imran glanced at him as he settled down and complimented him on the pull shot he played in the match, as well as told him that his form was good. Inzamam couldn't tell if Imran was joking or not. That was all Imran said to Inzamam before falling asleep. Inzamam owes a lot to Imran and gives him credit for the support and confidence he offered him in the beginning of his career.

On the night before the semi-final, manager Intikhab Alam gave Inzamam two sleeping pills. Inzamam still chuckles about how he always slept well and never needed medication. However, the medicines had such a strong effect on Inzamam that he spent the entire night vomiting and not sleeping a wink. In the morning Inzamam felt completely dehydrated and extremely weak. He didn't have any energy to play and didn't want to enter the match not fully fit. However, the most serious issue at hand was telling the captain of his illness. Because he lacked the courage to tell Imran Khan, he asked Mushtaq to inform the captain of his inability to play. Imran patiently heard Mushtaq before turning to Inzamam and telling him that not playing was not an option. He went on to say that he could choose not to field but had to play in the match. During New Zealand's innings, Inzamam barely fielded. When Salim Malik was dismissed, Javed Miandad could be seen gesturing to the dressing room to send in Wasim Akram, but Imran backed Inzamam to bat in the crucial situation. Pakistan were in a precarious position, requiring 124 runs in about 15 overs. At the time, scoring at 8 runs per over was practically unthinkable.

Cometh the hour cometh the man; Inzamam smashed 60 runs in 37 balls to take Pakistan to victory. Finally, Inzamam had justified Imran's trust in his exceptional batting prowess. Imran was overjoyed and he hugged Inzamam as he entered the dressing room. It was the first of many brilliant innings Inzamam played for Pakistan.

While Inzamam was mostly calm and kept to himself, he did lose his cool once. During the Sahara Cup in Toronto, a rude spectator kept calling him 'Aloo.' He told the 12th man to get a bat before climbing into the stands and assaulting the spectator. The crowd intervened and separated the two, but Inzamam's behaviour cost him a couple of matches as well as a complaint being filed against him. Finally, an out-of-court settlement brought the case to a close.

How many people know that Inzamam was the one who discovered Rashid Khan? Inzamam was invited by

Afghanistan to coach their national team after retirement. He was informed by the team manager that Rashid Khan was an excellent leg spinner. But the selectors were sure that Rashid was no good. Inzamam told them that there was no harm in calling him to the nets. When Rashid Khan arrived for trials, Inzamam padded up to play him. Rashid was enticed by Inzamam with the promise of including him in the squad if he could dismiss him. Despite Rashid's best efforts, he was unable to get Inzamam out but impressed him with his amazing skill and variety. Later Rashid made his debut while Inzamam was the coach. Inzamam claims that Rashid has yet not utilised his immense skill as a batsman, and needs to bat in the Top 5. Given Inzamam's vast knowledge of the game, don't be surprised if Rashid bats at No. 3 or No. 4 in the future!

Chapter 12

Suicide Point

One thing that hasn't changed over time is players' unwillingness to field at "forward short leg". Everyone who plays cricket will concur that it is the most dangerous position to be on the cricket field. Great players have described it as suicide zone, and there have been incidents where players have been seriously injured. But the tragic death of Raman Lamba when the ball struck him on the head has to be the worst of them all.

Interestingly, forward short leg is a position occupied by one of the junior-most members of the team. And that has not changed over the years; even when Rahul Dravid made his debut for India, he was initially positioned at forward short leg. Of course, when he established himself as an important cog in the wheel, he moved into the slips and became India's top slip fielder during his era. While the risk of being hit is still quite high even today, adequate protective gear ensures that injuries are kept to a minimum. Even then, players are still reluctant to field at forward short leg.

Eknath Dhondu Solkar, who was affectionately referred to by his teammates as "Ekky", was one player who made this dangerous position his own. Solkar was a good all-rounder, an exceptionally confident player, and an excellent team man, making him a captain's dream. Whatever the captain demanded, Solkar never refused. He wasn't a particularly skilled batsman, but that didn't stop him from rising to any challenges that were presented to him. He even opened the innings for India in a Test match in England.

Solkar had imprinted the ""khadoos" ethos of Mumbai cricket, having learned the game in Mumbai's maidans. He could bowl both pace and spin, like the renowned West Indian Sir Garfield Sobers. In fact, some dubbed him a "poor man's Sobers". His superb fielding at forward short leg, though, overshadowed his batting and bowling. He took many great catches, adding to the effectiveness of the spin quartet.

Solkar had a disastrous start to his career as a batsman. He was out for zero in his debut against New Zealand in Hyderabad. He was upset, as expected, and was sitting in his hotel room with his roommate Vishwanath. Although he was in the squad, Vishwanath was yet to make his Test debut. To cheer him up, Vishwanath told him that it was okay to get out for a duck since many successful cricketers had done that on their debut. Vishwanath then gave him the names of the cricketers who were dismissed for zero in their debut innings. Of course, most of them were made-up names.

After a month, Vishwanath made his debut in Kanpur against Australia and also was dismissed for zero in his debut innings. The same evening, his roommate Solkar advised him not to worry and reminded him of what Vishwanath had told him a month before: there were many players who got a zero yet went on to achieve great success. He then repeated Vishwanath the same names he had given him a month before, but he finished the list with Eknath Solkar. Vishwanath smiled when he heard Solkar's name on the list. It seems to have worked since Vishwanath hammered a century in the second innings.

Solkar's journey to becoming a superb forward short leg fielder from the outfield is an intriguing one. In the 1969 Test match between India and Australia at the Feroz Shah Kotla, Solkar first gained attention as a forward short-leg fielder. It was the opening day of the Test match. The Australian captain, Bill Lawry, won the toss and chose to bat. Early in the innings, Erapalli Prasanna was brought into the attack. There were a few bat-pad chances of Ian Chappell and Doug Walters that went down because there was no one at forward short leg. Prasanna was convinced that if a fielder was placed at that position, he would get a wicket. He went up to his skipper, MAK Pataudi, and voiced his request.

Captain Pataudi first asked Ajit Wadekar, who was fielding at slips, to field at forward short leg but Wadekar refused politely. Pataudi then went to Venkat who was fielding at gully, but he too, like Wadekar, declined. Finally, Pataudi approached Abid Ali, who was fielding at backward short leg, and asked him the identical question he had asked Wadekar and Venkat. He too replied that he was comfortable in his current position. Prasanna and Pataudi were both frustrated. Nobody wanted to field at forward short leg for fear of getting hit. Keep in mind that there were no safety equipment like shin guards or helmets available at the time.

The drinks interval was a welcome break. While the players were sipping water, Eknath Solkar approached Pataudi and gently inquired whether he could field at forward short leg. Pataudi, with surprise written all over his face and in complete disbelief, told Solkar that he is more than welcome to field at short leg. Prasanna smiled widely as he saw the forward short leg position taken.

In his first over after drinks, Prasanna consumed the prize scalp of Doug Walters when he played forward only to be caught by Eknath Solkar. It was the beginning of Solkar's love affair with forward short leg. The rest, as they say, is history; he went on to become the best fielder in that precarious position. He grabbed 53 catches in 27 Test matches, at a staggering average of nearly two catches every Test match. No fielder in the world has been as effective as Solkar at that position to date.

The dismissal of Allan Knott at Oval in 1971 is a perfect example of Solkar's keen observational skills as a cricketer. Throughout the Series, Knott was a thorn in the flesh of the Indians. In the first innings, he had scored 90 runs. So it was critical to get him out for the Indians to win. As Knott walked into bat, Solkar informed Wadekar that he had seen Knott use the bails to mark his guard. Then he quietly asked Wadekar if taking the bails off the stumps and putting them in the pocket was against the rules of the game. Wadekar said that was fine, but instructed Solkar to place the bails back, once Knott had marked his guard. As expected, Knott took guard before turning back to pick up the bails but he was unable to find them. As a result, he had no choice but to mark the traditional way. Solkar then quietly placed the bails on the stumps. It seemed to have had a psychological effect on Knott, as he was dismissed after scoring just one run, brilliantly caught by Solkar off Venkat. With Knott gone, India were in the driver's seat. They went on to win the match and the Series, making them the first Indian team to achieve it in England.

His verbal tiff with Geoffrey Boycott is legendary. During the 1974 Series he got under the skin of the English opener. He even sledged Boycott, saying "I will out you bloody." These famous words have become a part of Indian cricket's folklore. After capturing Boycott's wicket, Solkar followed him and said, "Go and tell your aunty." Captain Ajit Wadekar, with whom Solkar had a special relationship, was perplexed by Solkar's comment and asked him what he meant. "Boycott's girlfriend is older than him", Solkar casually responded. He dismissed Boycott consecutively for three innings. Solkar first dismissed Boycott in the second innings against Yorkshire, and then got the better of him in both innings in the match between India and MCC, a few days later.

Boycott never felt that Solkar had the upper hand over him despite the fact that Solkar had dismissed him a few times. He believed his dismissals were due to his bad form rather than the competence of the left arm pacer.

Solkar was an endearing character. Sadly, he passed away in 2005 at the age of 57.

CHAPTER 13

THE UNKNOWN HERO

When it comes to complimenting a cricketer, Ian Chappell is notoriously frugal. However, Chappell is never short of words while praising Doug Walters. He holds Doug Walters in the highest regard as a batsman and a team man. Walters appeared to be a very easygoing player, but below the casualness was a tremendously gifted batsman who could devastate any bowling attack and set up the game for his team. To highlight how aggressive he was, he scored 100 runs in a single session three times during his career. Even today, it is difficult to score a hundred runs in a session; so Doug Walters was unquestionably an exceptional player.

At the loss of Greg Chappell's wicket in Perth during the 1974 Ashes Series, Walters walked in to bat a few minutes before tea. As the two batsmen crossed each other, Greg Chappell told Doug Walters that he could score a century in the last session. Walters was batting on 3 at tea. After the break, he started in his characteristic swashbuckling style, smashing boundaries as he pleased. According to Ian Chappell, "He might have been around 60 at the drinks break." As the 12th man was about to leave the dressing room to give Walters some water, Chappell urged him to ask Walters, "How was it going?" "I think I've got a chance", Walters told the 12th man. Walters' onslaught on the English bowlers continued. Finally, it came down to Bob Willis bowling the final over of the day. Walters was on 93 and needed 10 runs to reach 100 in a session, but he was not on strike. Back then, it was an 8 ball over. The over began with a leg bye off the first ball. Walters was now on strike. He attempted to pull the second ball, a short one, but it took the top edge of the bat and flew to the boundary over the wicket keeper's head. Now, 6 runs had to be scored in six balls. The Australian players in the dressing room thought it would be a cakewalk, but the next five balls were all dot balls. Walters now needed a six of the last ball to reach 100 runs in a session. The dressing room was still optimistic that Walters would succeed. Willis committed the cardinal mistake of bowling a short ball, and Walters was waiting for it. He slammed it into the stands and completed 100 runs in a single session.

Normally, the entire team would applaud the batsman as he enters the dressing room after a fantastic innings, but Ian Chappell told all the players to hide in the shower so that no one would be there when Walters and his partner Ross Edwards came in. The players heard the two batsmen enter the dressing room but didn't hear anything more. Five minutes later, a curious Chappell emerged from the shower and entered the dressing room. He was surprised to see Walters smoking nonchalantly. So, Chappell asked Edwards about Walters' reaction upon entering the dressing room. According to Edwards, Walters didn't really care that there was no one in the dressing room to applaud; instead, he simply removed his pads and gloves and lit a cigarette, as was his routine. He took both success and failure in his stride and that was his greatest virtue.

He enjoyed playing cricket but was not the most disciplined player in the team. He loved his drinks and would stay at the pub till the early hours of the morning. But he was not short of runs despite his lack of sleep.

On the night before the Test match in Christchurch in 1977, a few Australian players went out to the pub. One by one, they left for their rooms to get some sleep and prepare for the morning match. By the end, only Walters and manager Roger Wootten remained in the pub. Wootten left the bar at 4am, but Walters was still enjoying his drink. On his way to the room, Wootten knocked on Marsh's door and told him that Walters was still at the bar. Marsh assured the manager that it was normal for Walters and would have no effect on his batting. The seaming conditions greeted both sides as they arrived at the ground on the morning of the match. New Zealand won the toss and promptly sent Australia in to bat. As predicted, Australia struggled against the moving ball and were reduced to 112 for 4. In walked Doug Walters. He struggled to make contact with the ball at first. Later, he admitted that he couldn't see the ball, but he endured the discomfort. After reaching 20, his feet started to move freely, his timing returned, and runs came thick and fast. Australia lost Chappell and Marsh in quick succession just as they seemed to be gathering momentum. Gilmour then joined Walters at 208 for 6. Australia did not lose another wicket and finished the day at 345 for 6, with Walters unbeaten on 129 and Gilmour on 65.

Walters returned to the pub, this time with Gilmour, and drank until 4am. As a result, the manager got frustrated once again and knocked on Marsh's door to tell him about

Walters and Gilmour. Like the previous night, Marsh urged the manager to calm down and go to sleep, but the manager was obviously not ready to do so. Finally, after much assurance from Marsh, the manager retired to his room.

Day 2 began with Richard Hadlee showcasing his skill. Walters experienced starting problems, just like the day before. However, after he got accustomed to the light and conditions, he began decimating the bowling attack. He raced past 200 runs and was the last man out for 250. It was time to celebrate, and Walters did not want to miss out, so he went out for the third night in a row to celebrate his highest score.

Unlike most of the other players, Walters had no issues waiting for his turn to bat. He loved playing cards in the locker room until he had to put on his pads. After he had padded up, he would focus on the game. Having said that, he knew exactly what was going on in the middle even though he was playing cards. Without a doubt, he was highly gifted and had a great cricket mind. Everyone praised his tremendous stroke play, but few realised that his sense of humour was second to none.

After the underarm incident, another instance unfolded that perfectly captures his carefree mindset. The Australian changing room was deafeningly silent, with most players unhappy with Greg Chappell's decision to instruct Trevor Chappell to bowl underarm. Doug Walters popped the first bottle of beer, breaking the silence in the dressing room. He then went to Rodney Marsh and said, "What's the fuss about?" Marsh was taken aback by Walters' insensitive question. Marsh reminded Walters that they had just denied New Zealand winning the match by bowling an underarm, which was against the spirit of the game. In response, Walters suggested that the batsman should have hit a six of the underarm. He then calmly stated that the batsman should have planted his foot on the line of the ball. When the ball would have struck the foot, it would have risen high enough to be blasted out of the ground. Everyone in the dressing room was startled, and they asked Walters if he could hit an underarm delivery for a six. Walters replied in the affirmative. The players challenged Walters to put into action what he had just preached. Walters showed up early the next day at the nets. Allan Border rolled an underarm delivery, and Walter thrust his front foot forward, allowing the ball to hit his foot, and when it rose, he smacked it out of the ground, exactly as he mentioned the previous evening. After walking the talk, Walters strolled out of the field, into the dressing room, and began playing cards.

Ian Chappell describes Doug Walters as a freak. When he first began playing, the Australian media dubbed him "the next Bradman". Although he was unable to match Sir Donald Bradman's average, his aggressive batting helped Australia win a number of games. The names of the Chappell brothers, Lillee, Thomson and Marsh from the Australian squad of the 1970s were well known to cricket fans all over the world. Doug Walters is one player whose name should be mentioned in the same breath. He was a hero both on and off the field.

CHAPTER 14

WORLD BEATERS

Those who grew up watching cricket in the 1970s and 1980s will agree that the West Indies team of that period was the finest to ever grace the cricket field. They had flamboyant batsmen, fearsome bowlers, and fabulous fielders. Simply stated, they were invincible. No matter where they played, at home or away, they destroyed every opponent and delighted their supporters.

A very good team would typically have three or four match-winners, but Clive Lloyd's West Indies team had nearly eight players who were capable of winning the game on their own. With so much ability and quality in the team, they were miles ahead of the competition. It was well known to the opposing sides going into the contest that they had little chance of winning against the powerful West Indies. All they prayed for was to lose with grace.

Despite the fact that they were from different islands, the players had fantastic camaraderie and inspired one another to perform better. The team was outstanding, and there are some wonderful anecdotes.

1984, WACA (Perth). Kim Hughes won the toss and put West Indies to bat. Thanks to superb centuries from Larry Gomes and Jeff Dujon, West Indies scored 416 runs in the first innings. On Day 2, Australia had to negotiate 10-12 overs before play ended. However, they got off to a bad start, losing three wickets. Garner claimed two of them, while Marshall picked up one. On Day 3, Clive Lloyd continued with his two successful bowlers, with Garner bowling into the wind and Marshall bowling with the wind behind him. After bowling 2 overs, Garner went up to Lloyd and requested him for a change of end. Since Marshall was in the midst of his spell, Lloyd told Garner that he could bowl from the other end after Marshall finishes his spell. Garner agreed and Lloyd tossed the ball to Michael Holding. On that day, the spectators at WACA were treated to an incredible spell of fast bowling by Holding. He took six wickets for 21 runs in nine overs and blew away Australia for a paltry 71 runs. It goes without saying that Joel Garner was unable to bowl another ball during that innings. Each bowler in that West Indies team was of such high calibre that they were all capable of running through a side on their day. Since they shared wickets most of the time, it's hardly surprising that none of the original group, which included Roberts, Holding, Garner and Croft picked up 300 Test wickets.

Up until the middle of the 1990s, West Indies were blessed to have a large pool of fast bowlers at their service. Over the years, there have been debates about which of those mean bowlers was the fastest. They all bowled at around the same pace, but Jeff Dujon who kept wickets for a long time believes Patrick Patterson was the quickest. Dujon had not kept wickets while Roberts and Holding were at their peak, but it doesn't take anything away from Patterson. In addition to his fierce pace, Patterson was also temperamental, and the Australians got a taste of that in 1988 at the MCG. With West Indies 356 runs ahead, Patterson joined Gordon Greenidge. Even though he batted only for a short period of time before the West Indies declared their innings, the Australians managed to get under the skin of the big burly Jamaican. As the teams returned to the dressing room, Patterson, who was sitting next to Dujon, was clearly disturbed and furious. He abruptly got up from his chair and walked over to the Australian dressing room. Dujon followed him to make sure nothing untoward happens. Seeing Patterson in a fit of rage, the Australians went dead silent. Patterson looked around, and pointing to four Australians said, "You, you, you, and you… I'll kill you!" After saying that, he stormed out of the room.

Needless to say, the next day he bowled like a beast, taking 5 wickets for 39 runs. Australia were dismissed for just 114 runs, and West Indies romped home by 285 runs. Patterson only played in 27 matches, which obviously did not do justice to his talent. However, opposition batsmen won't be complaining.

Malcolm Marshall was making headlines everywhere he played in the early 1980s. Unlike other West Indian fast bowlers, he was short yet lightning quick. He had an extraordinary cricket mind. Marshall was given the responsibility of spearheading the pace attack when Holding, Roberts and Garner retired. Like many youngsters, Curtly Ambrose wanted to impress Marshall when he first joined the team.

Ambrose toured England in 1988. He had already made his ODI debut and was being mentioned as the fast bowler to carry on the legacy of the West Indies pace attack.

Ian Bishop was also in the squad but had not yet played any international match. As the team landed in England, the reporters asked Marshall about Ambrose. Marshall's response was that Ambrose is an upcoming fast bowler, but Bishop will be the holy tower of West Indies cricket. Ambrose did not feel good but realised that he had to earn the respect of the great man. In the next two years, Ambrose impressed Marshall with his skill and then the relationship completely changed. Marshall took Ambrose under his wings and taught him the nuances of fast bowling.

Ambrose once related an intriguing incident that revealed Malcolm Marshall's cricket acumen. It happened in 1991 in Edgbaston. The ball was swinging a lot, and Gooch was playing and missing Marshall all the time. Ambrose was enjoying the duel from mid-off. "How do you think I'm going to get him out?" Marshall questioned Ambrose. Ambrose responded that Gooch would edge and get caught behind. Marshall said that the ball was moving too much and that he would keep missing it all day. He then stated with great confidence that he would dismiss him by knocking out his stumps. Ambrose was surprised by Marshall's confidence of getting Gooch bowled. In fact he thought Marshall was insane. But after a few balls, he understood Marshall's brilliance. Marshall first delivered an out-swinger that beat Gooch and then he did it again before bowling a superb in-swinger. The ball slipped in between Gooch's bat and pad and knocked the stumps out of the ground. Ambrose realised that Marshall had a phenomenal cricket brain. Marshall was without a doubt the best bowler that the West Indies produced, according to Ambrose.

Malcolm Marshall sadly passed away in 1999 at the age of 41 from colon cancer.

Joel Garner was one bowler who was really difficult to score against. He stood 6 feet 8 inches tall and had a very high action. This enabled him to generate significant bounce from even a docile wicket. He usually bowled short-of-length deliveries that ended up being chest-high, which made it exceedingly difficult for batsmen to score runs.

Here is an interesting conversation between Ian Botham and Geoff Boycott on how challenging it was to score runs against Garner. Botham and Garner were teammates in Somerset. In the team meeting prior to England's first match against Joel Garner, Geoff Boycott questioned Ian Botham over potential scoring opportunities against Garner. Botham stated that one couldn't hit Garner for runs, but rather push it away and pick up runs in singles and doubles. Boycott was not impressed by the response and questioned Botham how Richards played him in the nets. Botham said that nobody, not even the legendary Richards, dared to hit Garner.

Garner terrorised batsmen all over the world with his incredible yorkers. His unbelievable accuracy ensured that the tail-enders didn't last long. Big Bird, as he was fondly called, was a nice guy off the field.

West Indies used to be a powerhouse that dominated cricket for decades, but since the turn of the century, their performance has been rapidly declining. Even if the current West Indies squad was half as good as Clive Lloyd's team, the world would be treated to some spectacular cricket.

CHAPTER 15

HOWZATT?

Harold Dennis Bird, better known as Dickie Bird, is a well-known and respected umpire in the cricket world. He officiated in Test matches between 1973 and 1996, during a time when there were many tough cricketers to contend with. While he was friendly with the players, he made certain that discipline was upheld and that no one went overboard. He was an extremely popular umpire among the players, and they trusted his decisions without batting an eyelid.

Dickie Bird began his cricket career with Barnsley Club as an opening batsman, sharing the dressing room alongside Geoffrey Boycott and Michael Parkinson. Parkinson became a well-known journalist, while Boycott went on to become one of England's top openers. Dickie Bird vividly recalls the evening following practice when he, Parkinson, and Boycott were chatting at the edge of the boundary when Boycott firmly stated that he will play for England by the age of 23. He was just 14 at the time, but a few months before turning 24, he did play for England.

Dickie Bird's stint at Yorkshire was cut short because the team had a few openers, including Ken Taylor, a regular opener for the English team. Dickie Bird was unfortunately dropped after scoring an unbeaten 181 when Taylor returned from his international obligations. Before moving to Leicestershire, he played a few games in the middle order. He had his moments of glory in his new county and established himself as a regular member of the team. Dickie Bird's lack of form and persistent knee problems forced him to retire after a few years.

Dickie Bird began umpiring with trepidation. The first Test match he officiated was in 1973, just three years after making his debut as a county umpire. According to Charles Elliot, the other umpire who stood alongside Dickie Bird in his first Test, Dickie Bird was nervous in the umpire's room before the start of play. Elliot was concerned about Dickie Bird's ability to handle the pressure of Test cricket after seeing his anxiety. But Dickie Bird's outstanding LBW decision in the first Test match dispelled all of his concerns. The batsman was none other than England captain Ray Illingworth. Charles Elliot, who was standing at square leg, was astonished when Dickie Bird raised his finger in response to an appeal by New Zealand pace bowler Bruce Taylor, who was bowling around the wicket. When Elliot returned to the pavilion, he viewed the replay and was convinced that Dickie Bird had indeed made the correct decision. It goes without saying that making a difficult decision requires a great deal of self-confidence and presence of mind, yet Dickie Bird managed to do it in his very first Test match. That judgement convinced Elliot that Dickie Bird would be an excellent umpire in the future. He was spot on, as Dickie Bird would go on to become the world's best umpire in the ensuing years.

Bowlers would try their luck with Dickie Bird at times, but none could persuade him to change his mind. Here's an amazing story of how he stood his ground against Dennis Lillee. The big Australian fast bowler was brilliant at his craft but stubborn and belligerent. Dennis Lillee once felt the ball had lost its shape and demanded that it be replaced in the middle of an over. Dickie Bird politely told him that he will examine the ball at the end of the over. Lillee was trying to make his case very strongly since he didn't appreciate Dickie Bird's answer. The play was halted, so Ian Chappell approached them and enquired as to the reason for the stoppage. "Captain, your fast bowler wants me to replace the ball now, and I've told him that I'll look at it at the end of the over, but I won't be changing it now", Dickie Bird said. When Chappell saw Dickie Bird was not going to budge, he instantly asked Lillee to resume bowling. Lillee made his displeasure apparent by bowling off spin for the remainder of the over. Dickie Bird, as promised, asked for the ball at the end of the over.

Being a perfectionist, Dickie Bird wouldn't allow anything to hamper with the game's smooth operation. In the centenary Test match between England and Australia at Lords, the overnight rain had left the outfield soggy, so the two umpires - Dickie Bird and David Constant - refused to commence play. Both umpires went out several times to inspect the ground conditions, but because Dickie Bird wanted the field to be completely dry, the start was delayed. It clearly infuriated MCC members who believed the outfield was dry enough to play, and they assaulted David Constant in the Long Room when he returned to the pavilion after inspecting the pitch. Fortunately for Dickie Bird, he was still on the ground inspecting the outfield. The timely intervention of both captains - Greg Chappell and Ian Botham - saved the situation from getting out of hand. When the game eventually resumed, the umpires were escorted onto the field by the police.

In another case, Dickie Bird took the West Indies team off the field when Curtly Ambrose complained that the run-up was soaked in water. Dickie Bird, apparently furious, blamed the issue on a clogged drainage pipe as he walked back to the pavilion. However, the secretary of the Yorkshire Cricket Club, in a neatly worded press statement, denied any drainage pipe being clogged and stated that it was an unfortunate accident. It was later discovered that a drainage pipe had broken, causing water to ooze to the ground's surface. After a few hours, when Dickie Bird thought the ground was completely dry, the game finally started.

Dickie Bird eventually took the decision to retire after 66 Test matches over a 23-year period. He chose the second Test match between England and India at Lords as his final Test as an umpire. Both teams formed a corridor and gave Dickie Bird a guard of honour as he walked out at the start of play on Day 1. It was the first time a player or an umpire had experienced such a gesture from the players. Dickie Bird was moved and took his position at the bowler's end with misty eyes, but it didn't stop him from adjudicating Mike Atherton out LBW on the fifth ball of Srinath's opening over. In fact, the Test match is remembered for Sourav Ganguly's debut century and Rahul Dravid's spirited 96.

Dickie Bird has been asked many times who he thinks is the finest batsman having watched several fine cricketers from the best seat in the house. He certainly holds Vivian Richards, Sunil Gavaskar, Martin Crowe, and Greg Chappell in high regard. But it was Barry Richards who left an indelible mark on him. However when it came to the best all-rounder ever, Dickie Bird didn't hesitate for a second, replying, "Sir Garfield Sobers." Dickie Bird describes Sobers as someone who could do anything on the cricket field. Sobers and Dickie Bird had and still do have a great deal of admiration for one another.

The first ball to leave Shane Warne's hand on English soil mesmerized the world. The umpire at the bowling end, Dickie Bird, had the best view of the magic ball. He recollects the ball started to drift sideways before pitching outside the leg stump, then spun across the face of the bat and clipped the off stump. Dickie Bird says that he has seen some spectacular deliveries by some fantastic bowlers over his long career as an umpire, but nothing compares to Warne's 'ball of the century'. While Warne's magic stunned Mike Gatting, Dickie Bird was dazzled as well, but recalls telling Warne immediately after the delivery, "Young man, you'll put your name in the record books." Dickie Bird predicted correctly. Shane Warne made history and rose to prominence as the best leg spinner in the world.

The phone rang at Dickie Bird's house on a terrible chilly day. The caller identified himself as the Master of Household from Buckingham Palace. He said that the Queen of England had commanded him to see whether Dickie Bird was available for lunch. Though Dickie Bird wasn't fully convinced that the call was genuine, he didn't want to miss lunch with the Queen of England, so he accepted the invitation. He was supposed to arrive at 1pm, but he arrived at the Buckingham Palace gates at 8am, five hours early. The guards informed him that he was too early and would have to wait until the Change of Guard. With plenty of time on his hands, Dickie Bird spent 4 hours in a local coffee shop before entering the palace at 1pm. The Queen came on time, and to Dickie Bird's astonishment, there was no other guest for lunch with the Queen. They had a lovely conversation that began over lunch and lasted until late afternoon. Dickie Bird considers it to be the most memorable day of his life.

Dickie Bird was a charming person both on and off the field. Even if he made a mistake, he was able to recover before the next ball. All over the world, fans still admire Dickie Bird for his wit and humour. A true legend in the world of cricket.

Chapter 16

Warne Tames his Rockstar

While Australia never believed in giving Shane Warne the captaincy, Rajasthan Royals did, and he demonstrated his brilliant skills as a captain in the very first edition of the IPL. The Royals lineup lacked big names, but there were some young, talented players. The team required a leader to guide and motivate them. And no one was better suited for the job than Warne.

Among the talented members of the team was a young man named Ravindra Jadeja, who had caught Shane Warne's eye. Jadeja had impressed Warne with his talent and energy. However, Jadeja's lack of discipline had irritated Warne on a few occasions.

Ravindra Jadeja failed to board the team bus as it was about to leave for practice one day. Seizing the opportunity to teach the youngster a lesson, Warne directed the bus driver to leave for the ground and instructed the hotel staff to notify Jadeja to arrive at the practice session as soon as possible by arranging his own transportation.

Jadeja made it to the ground and joined the training session. After a long session, all the players were relaxing in the coach on their way back from the ground. Shane Warne stopped the bus just before the hotel and asked Ravindra Jadeja to get off and walk to the hotel. Everyone thought Warne was joking at first, but soon realised he was dead serious. A stunned Jadeja received support from another teammate who attempted to explain the reason for the delay. Warne bowled another googly by instructing the other player also to accompany Jadeja to the hotel. They both got off the bus and walked to the hotel, where they rejoined their teammates.

Following that incident, Jadeja was never late for a practice session and displayed no lack of discipline. Jadeja and Warne had enormous mutual respect for each other, and this incident had no impact on their relationship. Shane Warne used to refer to Jadeja as his "Rockstar".

CHAPTER 17

CRICKET'S 'BLACK DAY'

There have been numerous controversies that have engulfed the cricketing world. The most contentious would be the Bodyline Series, but the infamous underarm delivery would not be far behind. Cricketers, fans, and just about everyone who follows this magnificent game have had discussions on this incident at least a couple of times. However, not a single person would approve of Australian skipper Greg Chappell's strategy. Of course, Chappell came to regret his decision, which is not surprising, but the reason behind it is intriguing.

Greg Chappell had an outstanding performance in the match with both the bat and the ball. He bowled his quota of 10 overs and took three wickets after scoring 90 runs. It was a blistering hot Sunday at the MCG, and the players' energy was dwindling with each passing minute. It was the third of the best-of-five finals. Australia had won the first two finals; and if they won the third final, the fourth and the fifth finals, which were scheduled for Tuesday and Thursday, would not have to be played. Greg Chappell was desperate to win the third final, and get enough rest for the Test match on Saturday.

In fact Greg Chappell wanted to leave the field around the 40th over because he was completely exhausted; but Rod Marsh insisted that he stayed because Marsh believed the match could go down to the wire. Chappell reluctantly agreed.

New Zealand needed 15 runs with 4 wickets in hand going into the final over. Richie Benuad believes Greg Chappell miscalculated so badly that Dennis Lillee, his leading fast bowler, bowled the penultimate over rather than the final over. Greg was forced to toss the ball to Trevor Chappell. Richard Hadlee was on strike and smashed the first ball to the boundary. 11 runs were needed from 5 balls. Hadlee appeared to be taking New Zealand to victory, but he was out caught on the second ball of the over. Ian Smith came in and got right into the action, scoring two runs off the third and fourth balls. 6 off 2 appeared to be anyone's game but Trevor Chappell clean bowled Ian Smith with the penultimate ball of the match.

Greg Chappell was sitting on the ground with his arms around the knees as Brian McKechnie made his way to the middle. At that point, Greg Chappell recalled Wayne Daniel smashing a six on the last ball of a World Series Cricket match, stealing the game away from Australia. He clearly did not want history to be repeated; so he walked up to Trevor Chappell and asked him "How you bowling your underarm?" It took Trevor by surprise and he replied "I don't know." Greg shot back "Well, you are just gonna find out, aren't ya?" Greg walked up to the umpire and informed him to notify the batsman that Trevor would be bowling underarm.

As Trevor rolled the ball underarm, the batsman blocked it and flung his bat in disdain. Greg Chappell's decision was not appreciated by anyone including his teammates. When the Australians started to walk back to the pavilion, the crowd began to boo them.

While Richie Benaud called it "disgraceful performance" and added that "it was one of the worst things I've seen on the cricket field", the New Zealand Prime Minister said the ball was an "act of true cowardice and I consider it appropriate that the Australian team were wearing yellow."

However, in the aftermath of this terrible incident, the International Cricket Council (ICC) changed the rule to state that an underarm delivery is illegal unless otherwise agreed before the match. What happened on February 1, 1981 will never be forgotten.

CHAPTER 18

PRICELESS KIWI

There have been many excellent batsmen over the last 4 decades, but only a few of them have made the audience drop their jaws. Martin Crowe from New Zealand was one of them. He was a great batsman during his time, but never got his due. With his skill and ability, he should be the first choice in most World XI selected by ex-cricketers, but he isn't in any of them. It was probably the disadvantage of playing for a team that dominated at home but struggled to win abroad.

The riveting contest between the ageing Andy Roberts and an emerging Martin Crowe was one of the most talked about incidents on the county circuit in the 1980s. Roberts was playing for Leicestershire, while Crowe was representing Somerset. Roberts had already played his final Test match but still had the pace to intimidate batsmen and had a successful season, taking many wickets. The greenish wicket at Taunton meant he would be more than a handful.

Leicestershire won the toss and elected to bat first, scoring 254. Somerset were struggling at 97 for 5 on Day 2 with Roberts taking three wickets with his away-going cutters. The only batsman standing between Leicestershire and a big first innings lead was Martin Crowe. He had a string of very good scores leading up to the match, so his confidence was sky-high. Crowe always knew where his off-stump was, so he left Andy Roberts' away-going deliveries, forcing the West Indian to bowl straighter, allowing him to work the ball away for runs.

Andy Roberts got infuriated by Crowe's defiance, and he began to crank up pace and go for the batsman's torso. As the teams returned to the pavilion for lunch, Crowe had to be treated for his bruises. After lunch, Crowe decided to go after Roberts and began playing horizontal shots to the balls that were short. It simply prompted Roberts to bowl faster and go after Crowe. The batsman was in danger of being injured as the conflict became more intense. On two consecutive deliveries he swayed away from the line, but he was ready for the next one that was pitched up by Roberts, and he smashed it over the bowler's head to the boundary.

The next two balls were bowled by Roberts with the intention of injuring Crowe rather than getting him out. He consciously overstepped and went wide to bowl on the batsman's body. Crowe claims that he saw the most enraged eyes in a bowler during those two balls. Crowe escaped Roberts' wrath, but the rest of his colleagues were unable to stand up to him, and Roberts ended up with seven wickets.

Somerset required 314 runs to win, but they got off to a poor start. They were 3 for 2 at lunch. Crowe began to play some magnificent strokes after lunch, and the crowd in Taunton was treated to an absolutely delightful performance of outstanding batting. Crowe continued to play his whole repertoire of shots despite Roberts' aggressive bowling. Crowe seemed unfazed by any bowler, smashing each one with ease. He made a superb 190 and was bowled when Somerset required just 2 runs to win. Leicestershire, the table-toppers, were defeated by Somerset in the end. Crowe emerged as a champion batsman over the next few years, scoring runs against every opposition team and laying claim to being the best batsman in the world.

Crowe had a brilliant cricket mind. As a captain, he was innovative, and we were fortunate to witness that in full glory during the 1992 World Cup. Crowe set the trend that captains in the T20 format follow today by opening the bowling with an off spinner - which was unheard of at the time. Opening the batting with a middle-order batsman like Greatbatch, who was not known for his strokeplay, was a brilliant move that paid off handsomely.

Despite making a brilliant century, Crowe was unable to lead New Zealand to the 1992 World Cup final. He was injured while batting and was unable to take the field. He sat in the changing room and helplessly watched as Pakistan defeated New Zealand in the semi-final. It was the most regrettable day of his life.

Crowe passed away in 2016 after a battle with cancer. With his understanding of the game, he would have been invaluable to New Zealand cricket.

CHAPTER 19

SOS, COLIN COWDREY!

The Australian tearaway fast bowlers Dennis Lillee, Jeff Thomson and Max Walker destroyed England in Brisbane. They were fast, ruthless, and hostile, and playing them was nothing short of a nightmare. After losing the first Test match in Brisbane, England faced a major problem when Dennis Amiss and John Edrich were injured and unable to play in the second Test. England desperately needed a batsman to stop Australia's rampant pace attack.

Colin Cowdrey had retired from Test cricket four years ago. While watching the Ashes Series from his armchair at home in Kent during the cold winter of England, he never imagined he would be called up to play for England again. He played Wes Hall and Charlie Griffith, Ray Lindwall and Keith Miller, Peter Heine and Neil Adcock with confidence, courage, and success due to his impeccable technique against pace bowling. Mike Denness was a big fan of Colin Cowdrey and thought he could stop Australia's pace attack.

On the last day of the Brisbane Test, Cowdrey received a call from Mike Denness asking if he was ready to battle in Australia, to which he replied, "I'd love to!" He packed his cricket equipment into the coffin, boarded a plane, flew for 47 hours, and arrived in Perth. He had net sessions the next few days, either early morning or late evening to avoid the scorching heat of the sun, and a few slip catching sessions while wearing gloves to protect his fingers.

On the first morning of the Test match, Colin Cowdrey walked in to bat after Ian Chappell won the toss and chose to field. Cowdrey's only preparation consisted of three hours of net practice. As he came into bat, the crowd was unsure whether the retired overweight English legend could keep up with Lillee and Thomson's ferocious pace.

Thomson unleashed a devastating delivery that soared dangerously over the batsman's head, bouncing once before hitting the sight-screen, giving Rod Marsh no chance to catch it. Cowdrey was at the non-striker's end when Thomson made eye contact with him as he turned to return to the top of his run up. The English batsman calmly extended his hand, and said, "Good morning, I'm Cowdrey." While Thomson shook Cowdrey's hand, he later admitted that no one had ever done something like that to him and thought to himself, "Good luck if you think that's going to do you any good."

Cowdrey took some body blows but did not cringe. He stood like a rock and to a large extent his impeccable technique helped him. He eventually fell after scoring 22 runs but not before occupying the crease for 2 hours. Cowdrey opened in the second innings as Lackhurst was injured. He was fortunate to be dropped by Ross Edwards and the ball teased the slip fielders on a few occasions. Cowdrey survived a confident appeal on 37 but he was unable to capitalise on the reprieve. He was caught plumb in front of the wicket by a fast delivery from Jeff Thomson after reaching 41. It was his highest score in the Series, but more importantly, he batted for more than four hours in the Test match with grit and determination.

Cowdrey could not change England's fortune in the Series, as Australia annihilated England 4-1 and won the Ashes, but he showed the world that even at 42, he had the courage to face the world's best fast bowlers.

Chapter 20

Boom Boom was Born

Pakistan arrived in Nairobi for the four-nation tournament, but suffered a major setback when ace leg spinner Mushtaq Ahmed was injured. Pakistan were desperately looking for a wrist spinner when the team management was informed of a youngster who was touring the West Indies with the Pakistan A side. Shahid Afridi was that young man. He received an SOS to join the Pakistan team right away.

As he began his journey to Nairobi, Afridi was both excited and nervous. He flew from Guyana to Barbados, then to Jamaica, and finally to Karachi via London and Dubai. He didn't sleep a wink the entire flight because he was overjoyed to have been chosen for Pakistan. Within a few hours of arriving in Karachi, he boarded the flight to Nairobi. Afridi recalls the seniors in the team being extremely friendly to him, particularly captain Wasim Akram.

For the first time, Afridi demonstrated his batting skills in the nets. After all of the regular batsmen had finished their innings, Akram and Waqar began bowling spin to the bowlers who had padded up. Then Akram asked Afridi if he could bat. Afridi responded confidently and positively. They were taken aback when they saw Afridi effortlessly hit the ball out of the ground. It didn't matter because both fast bowlers were bowling spin, but the lack of effort and the distance the ball travelled off Afridi's bat impressed them.

The next day, Akram told Afridi to bat while the ball was still relatively new, and both he and Waqar were fresh. Afridi treated both of them in the same manner as the previous evening. Akram recognised Afridi's potential right away. Unfortunately, Akram's father suffered a heart attack and he had to rush home, but he told the stand-in captain Ramiz Raja to keep Afridi in mind and send him up the order.

Shahid Afridi was so excited the night before Pakistan's match against Sri Lanka that he woke up at 1am and got ready without realising the time. Only when Shadab Kabir, his roommate, told him the time did Afridi go back to sleep again. He told Shadab the next morning that he had dreamt about hitting Jayasuriya, Dharmasena and Muralitharan for sixes. "Let's hope it happens," Kabir said as they left for the ground.

Pakistan's match against Sri Lanka was crucial because Pakistan needed to win big in order to qualify for the final. Pakistan batted first after Sri Lanka won the toss and chose to field. Ramiz Raja the stand-in captain sent in Shahid Afridi after they lost opener Salim Elahi. It was a brilliant move, as Afridi smashed 11 sixes and 6 fours in the next 37 balls to set a world record for the fastest century. Pakistan went on to win by a huge margin and advance to the final.

Interestingly, Afridi used Sachin Tendulkar's bat to create the world record. But how did Afridi get his hands on Sachin's bat? Back then, even Indian cricketers got their bats from across the border, and Sialkot was a haven for bats. Sachin had given Waqar a sample bat and asked him to order identical bats. Just before the match, Waqar handed Afridi the sample bat and urged him to use it.

As they say, the rest is history. Afridi had a glorious career and achieved the success that only few could achieve on the international stage. For someone who began his career as a bowler, Afridi evolved into an intimidating batsman who instilled fear in the opposition. Surely, the bat must be sitting proudly in Afridi's home, alongside the numerous trophies he has won around the world.